T0197902

Rastafari: A Very Short Introduction

VERY SHORT INTRODUCTIONS are for anyone wanting a stimulating and accessible way into a new subject. They are written by experts, and have been translated into more than 45 different languages.

The series began in 1995, and now covers a wide variety of topics in every discipline. The VSI library now contains over 500 volumes—a Very Short Introduction to everything from Psychology and Philosophy of Science to American History and Relativity—and continues to grow in every subject area.

Titles in the series include the following:

Ennis B. Edmonds

RASTAFARI

A Very Short Introduction

OXFORD
UNIVERSITY PRESS

OXFORD
UNIVERSITY PRESS

Great Clarendon Street, Oxford, OX2 6DP,
United Kingdom

Oxford University Press is a department of the University of Oxford.
It furthers the University's objective of excellence in research, scholarship,
and education by publishing worldwide. Oxford is a registered trade mark of
Oxford University Press in the UK and in certain other countries

© Ennis B. Edmonds 2012

The moral rights of the author have been asserted

First Edition published in 2012

British Library Cataloguing in Publication Data

Data available

ISBN 978-0-19-958452-9

Printed and bound by
CPI Group (UK) Ltd, Croydon, CR0 4YY

*To the pioneers of Rastafarian studies who are no
longer with us: Leonard E. Barrett, Carole Yawney,
Rex Nettleford, and my dear friend and colleague,
Barry Chevannes*

Contents

List of illustrations

Introduction: comprehending Rastafari

While some are repulsed by the reputed copious ganja (marijuana) smoking and gorgon-like hairstyle of Rastas, others are attracted by the anti-establishment impulse they have come to represent. But often, the casual observer makes no further inquiry into and has no comprehension of the foundational drive behind Rastafari. However, to understand Rastafari, we must understand and appreciate that it arose from, on the one hand, a decisive rejection of the hegemonic and homogenizing British imperial culture that dominated Jamaica's colonial society, and, on the other, a determined effort to fashion an identity that is based on the re-appropriation of an African heritage. For 'those who have ears to hear', Bob Marley expresses this categorical rejection of Babylon (Western society with its alienating and oppressive institutions and values) in the opening words of 'Babylon System': 'We refuse to be, what you wanted us to be / We are what were; and that's the way it's going to be'. As alienated and marginalized people trapped in the underside of Jamaica's colonial society, the early Rastas drew inspiration from the crowning of Haile Selassie I, looking to sever cultural and psychological ties to the British colonial society, which for centuries had disparaged African traditions and sought to inculcate European mores in Jamaicans of African descent. Furthermore, the early Rastas made the newly crowned potentate the symbol of their positive affirmation of Africa as the source of their spiritual and cultural heritage.

1

Both Rastas and scholars who study the Rastafari movement affirm that beyond the obvious symbols and practices of Rastafari, the question of identity stands at the core of the movement. In his book, *Rastafari: For the Healing of the Nation*, Rastafarian devotee Dennis Forsythe asserts that Rastafari is a grassroots movement whose major focus is posing and responding to 'the fundamental cultural and human question, Who am I? or What am I?'. Behavioral scientist, business consultant, farmer, and Rastafarian visionary Leahcim Semaj (Michael James in reverse) concurs with Forsythe in a journal article entitled, 'Race and Identity and Children of the African Diaspora: Contributions of Rastafari'. Reflecting on Rastafari's refusal to imbibe an imposed European cultural identity, Semaj declares that Rastafari proposes a more 'attainable and psychologically healthy answer to the question of WHO AM I'. Rex Nettleford, the foremost scholar of Caribbean society and culture from the 1960s till his passing in 2010, aptly sums up the identity question at the heart of Rastafari in *Mirror Mirror* by describing Rastas as those who are 'liberated from the obscurity of themselves'.

Not surprising, therefore, is the Rastafarian emphasis on the 'I' as the philosophical foundation of the identity of its devotees. By utilizing 'I' to denote Rastafarian consciousness of the self as divine, Rastafari elevates its most socially marginalized adherents to a status that highlights their position next to Jah (God). Since 'I' indicates their consciousness of the 'godness' that inheres in the self, they boldly affirm their physical characteristics, African past, and creative ability to fashion their own culture to mirror their sense of self. Rastafarian tenets, practices, and symbols are all the exterior articulation of this sense of self. Ganja smoking, for example, is a vehicle that conveys Rastas through the alienating mental maze that Babylon has created and returns them to the consciousness of self as the divine-infused children of God. Dreadlocks are the multivalent symbol of Rastafarian self-confidence, valorization of African beauty, and mystical connection with Jah. The principles of Rastafarian lifestyle, called 'livity', encode a commitment to live organically and harmoniously with the environment, which is infused with Jah's power.

Though Rastafari has traveled far from it roots in Jamaica and has attracted followers who do not share the same ethnic heritage and social history as the people of African descent who first forged the movement, the essential core of Rastafari as consciousness of one's divine identity still remains. Many people of all ethnic stripes, who find themselves marginalized by what they perceive as the oppressive and homogenizing values and institutions of their society, have found in Rastafari a means of resisting those values and institutions, and returning home to a sense of self, rooted in a divine relationship with Jah.

Chapter 1, '"Movement of Jah people": the history of Rastafari in Jamaica', traces Rastafari from its emergence in the colonial outpost of Jamaica to its present entrenchment in Jamaican society as a potent social and cultural force. It discusses the appearance of itinerant preachers declaring Haile Selassie as the divine black liberator shortly after his coronation in 1930; the rise in the 1940s of a radical cadre of young Rastas, House of Youth Black, who were responsible for instituting some of the enduring features of the movement; the heightened conflicts with the Jamaican establishment of the 1950s and 1960s; the changing circumstances and status of Rastafari in the late 1960s and 1970s; the lull in Rastafarian militancy in the 1980s; and its resurgence since the mid-1990s.

Chapter 2, '"Rastatology" and "livity": the principles and practices of Rastafari', examines the worldview, symbols, and lifestyle of Rastafari. More specifically, it discusses the major tenets of Rastafari: the experience of being in exile in 'Babylon'; consciousness of self as divine, deification of Haile Selassie; and repatriation to Ethiopia/Africa as the Promised Land. The chapter also examines the major elements of Rastafarian lifestyle: dreadlocks, ganja smoking, reasoning, dreadtalk, and ital cuisine.

In Chapter 3, 'Grounding, houses, and mansions: social formation of Rastafari', the focus turns to how the Rastafarian ethos works to fashion and maintain Rastafarian identity, and how fluidity and multiple formations are characteristic of the movement as a whole. In this respect, the chapter discusses the concept of 'grounding' which indicates the ritual and social activities that establish and sustain one's consciousness as Rastafari. The chapter also profiles the major sects of Rastafari: Nyabinghi, the strict, traditional culture of Rastafari that proscribes any compromise with the forces of Babylon; Twelve Tribes of Israel, which assumes the identity of the ancient Hebrews and whose members are more likely to engage with the world of Babylon; and Bobo Shanti (also Bobo Dreads), followers of the charismatic Prince Emmanuel who are mostly associated with their commune in Bull Bay, Jamaica, and who are recognized by their flowing white robes and colourful head wraps; Abuna Foxe's Church of Haile Selassie and Rastafari Theocratic Government; and Fulfilled Rastafari, an international, multicultural group of Rastas that has emerged in recent years.

Focusing on the means by which Rastafari have become an international movement, Chapter 4, 'Rastafari international: the making of a global movement', explores the spread of Rastafari throughout the Caribbean, to Caribbean immigrant communities in Europe and North America, to African diasporic people and Africans on the continents, and to people of disparate ethnicities in the Americas, Europe, and Asia. The chapter highlights the migration of Jamaicans, including Rastas, to North America, Europe, and Africa, the spreading of the message of Rastafari through reggae music, and the travelling missions of 'trodding' Rastafarian elders to inculcate Rastafarian principles and practices in adherents outside Jamaica.

Chapter 5, 'Kingmen, queens, and dawtas: gender issues in Rastafari' tackles the contentious issue of the patriarchal ideology and gender inequality in Rastafari. Rastafari is a male redemption movement seeking to rehabilitate diasporic African males from the emasculation of slavery and colonialism. In doing so, it has promulgated a discourse and promoted the practice of female subjugation. However, women in Rastafari have eked out spaces of self-empowerment and have increasingly challenged their prescribed roles within the movement.

Despite its humble beginnings, Rastafari has become a creative force influencing cultural production in Jamaica and beyond. Chapter 6, '"The head corner stone": Rastafari and Caribbean culture', takes up and explores the influence of Rastafari on contemporary Caribbean culture. Rastafari's role in the development and dissemination of Jamaican popular music and its impact on the evolution of visual arts since the 1960s illustrates this influence most readily. But Rastafari extends its influence to the literary arts of contemporary Caribbean fiction and poetry writing, performing arts, and the arts and crafts sold to tourists as emblematic of Caribbean culture.

Out of the dark colonial past of their forbears, Rastas have risen up to affirm their self-dignity, African heritage, and right to self-determination. In so doing, they have shown us that the most marginalized group of people can rise up to resist the most entrenched power structure. And from the margins of society can come a burst of energy and creativity that can have ripple effects in that society and around the world. Bob Marley captures well the trajectory of Rastafari, from being the children of an enslaved people to making a significant mark on the world. In his/her most celebrated ballad, 'Redemption Song', he sings,

> Old pirates, yes, the rob I, Sold I to the merchant ships.
> Minutes after they took I, from the bottomless pit.
> But my hand was made strong, by the hand the Almighty.
> We forward in this generation triumphantly.

Chapter 1

'Movement of Jah people': the history of Rastafari in Jamaica

The appearance of self-appointed preachers on the streets of Jamaica in the early 1930s proclaiming a new message was not of itself remarkable. Jamaica was well steeped in the tradition of charismatic preachers roaming the streets and proclaiming divine messages, at least since the historic religious awakening of 'The Great Revival' of the 1860s. This decade saw a great stirring of spiritual interest and excitement in the Christian churches. But the most enduring outcome was the emergence of the African-Christian tradition popularly known as Revivalism (or Revival Zion), whose leaders and followers made holding 'open air' meetings at crossroads and in village centres an essential part of their religious activity. Furthermore, most Jamaican communities had encounters with the 'warner', a Revivalist visionary who periodically wandered through a district or from district to district warning of some impending catastrophe and encouraging his hearers to repent. However, these 1930s preachers came with a dramatic difference. They were strident and vehement in their condemnation of Jamaica's colonial government and society, and they were proclaiming that Christ had reappeared in the person of the recently crowned emperor of Ethiopia, Haile Selassie, who they claimed would bring an end to white domination and the exploitation of black people around the world.

How these early bearers of the message of Rastafari arrived at this conclusion is somewhat complicated, but it was the convergence of several religious, cultural, and intellectual streams. The local stream is the influence of Jamaica's vernacular religious culture, with its history of resistance to British hegemony and its appropriation of the biblical messianism leading to an expectation of a future liberator who would bring an end to the oppression and marginalization of blacks everywhere. Another stream is the African diaspora identification with Ethiopia as a symbol of black identity and hope of liberation. Probably the most immediate and powerful stream is the Garvey movement of the 1910s and 1920s that rallied grassroots support for Ethiopianism and Pan Africanism in black communities across the world. Marcus Garvey's emphases on black pride, repatriation, and self-reliance have become salient elements of Rastafari. Garvey (see Figure 1) himself has been accorded the status of a prophet in Rastafari, and his purported prophecy of the crowning of an African king as a sign of black liberation was the trigger that propelled some of his followers to identify Haile Selassie as the messiah. A less recognized but nevertheless important stream was a rise in black consciousness and black activism throughout the Americas (as well as Africa) after World War I. Rastafari is part of the same cultural wave of the 1920s and 1930s that produced the Harlem Renaissance, the *Indigenist* and *Noirist* movements in Haiti, *Afro-Cubanismo* in Cuba, *Consciência Negra* among black Brazilians, *Negritude* in the French Antilles, Paris, and West Africa, and a host of liberation and independence movements across Africa.

Thus, while Rastafari marks a distinctive development in Afro-Jamaican religiosity and struggle for self-definition, it falls within a venerable history of resistance to the hegemonic power of European politics, economics, and culture in Jamaica and the Africa diaspora. Hence when Ras Tafari was crowned as Haile Selassie I, Emperor of Ethiopia, many Jamaicans of African descent, with a history of resistance to white domination and attuned to black consciousness currents of the early 1900s, were disposed to find racial and religious significance in this historic event.

1. Statue of Marcus Garvey—in front of St Ann's Bay Library, in St Ann, Jamaica

Ethiopianism

Ethiopianism emerged as an intellectual and cultural movement among blacks in Africa and the diaspora during the 18th and 19th centuries. Through the excavation of a glorious African past, particularly the contributions of Ethiopia to early human civilization, Ethiopianism sought to expunge the idea of Africa as the 'dark continent' where nothing but barbarism had prevailed since the dawn of human history. By recalling the historical achievements of Africans, it drew inspiration from a glorious past and sustained the hope of a glorious future when Ethiopia would reclaim its place as a beacon of black civilization and when all Africa and Africans would be liberated from white domination. This movement inspired African-Americans and Africans to include the word 'African' or 'Ethiopian' in the names of their churches and other social organizations in the eighteenth and nineteenth centuries. His references to Ethiopia and those passages of the Bible that mention Ethiopia probably suggest that George Lisle, who brought the Baptist faith to Jamaica, was an Ethiopianist. The focus on Ethiopia by Rastafari is a legacy of Ethiopianism.

Founding fathers

In the years immediately following reports in the Jamaican press concerning Haile Selassie's coronation, which was attended by over 70 world dignitaries including Prince Edward (later King Edward VIII), a number of itinerant street preachers started appearing in Kingston and some rural areas proclaiming that Christ had returned in the person of Haile Selassie. Foremost among these were Leonard Percival Howell (see Figure 2), Joseph Nathaniel Hibbert (see Figure 3), Robert Hinds, and Henry Archibald Dunkley. Though all these founding Rastas had long careers and significant influence on the formation and growth of Rastafari, Howell soon became the public face of the movement

9

2. Leonard Howell, a founder of the Rastafari movement

and the main figure around whom the conflict between the new movement and the Jamaican establishment was played out until the mid-1950s.

From its very inception, and for the next 30 years, Rastafari existed in an increasingly conflictual relationship with Jamaican authorities, who employed repressive measures to contain the movement that it viewed as potentially disruptive to public peace. For their vitriol against the British colonial government then ruling Jamaica and for their insistence that Haile Selassie was the rightful monarch of black people, Joseph Hibbert, Archibald Dunkley, Robert Hinds, and Leonard Howell suffered police

3. Joseph Hibbert

surveillance, arrests, and imprisonment. As Howell projected
himself to the forefront of the movement, he became the focus of
state action against Rastafari. In December 1933, Howell and his
assistant Hinds took their revolutionary teachings to the parish
of St. Thomas, east of Kingston. There Howell asserted that
blacks were superior to whites; excoriated the colonial
government as illegitimate; declared Haile Selassie to be
the only ruler worthy of the allegiance of black people; urged the
cessation of the payment of taxes to the representatives of the
British crown; and called for an uprising against the white
oppressors. Probably remembering the blood bath of the Morant
Bay Rebellion in St. Thomas some 70 years earlier, the colonial

Founding Rastas

Among the itinerant street preachers who appeared in Kingston and some rural areas in the early 1930s proclaiming that Christ had returned in the person of Haile Selassie were Leonard Percival Howell, Joseph Nathaniel Hibbert, Robert Hinds, and Henry Archibald Dunkley. Born in 1898 in rural Jamaica, Howell travelled to and worked in Panama during his teens and early twenties. He apparently joined or worked for the United States transport service, leading to his travels to New York, where he settled after 1923 when he left the service. In New York, he was exposed to the black consciousness and black liberation ideas emanating from Marcus Garvey, figures in the Harlem Renaissance, and George Padmore, the communist theorist from Trinidad. Returning to Jamaica in 1932, Howell started proclaiming that Ras Tafari was the black messiah to whom the allegiance of the black race should be directed.

Hibbert had migrated from Jamaica to Costa Rica at the age of 17 in 1911 to work in the banana industry. From there he relocated to Colon, Panama, where many Jamaicans worked in the Canal Zone. While in Central America, Hibbert joined the Ancient Mystic Order of Ethiopia and eventually ascended to the position of Master Mason. Returning to Jamaica in 1931, he commenced declaring the divinity of Ras Tafari at about the same time as Howell, first in the rural areas of St. Andrew and shortly thereafter in Kingston.

Dunkley gained his international perspective through his travels as a sailor for the United Fruit Company. Disembarking in Port Antonio, Jamaica in December 1930, only a month after the coronation of Haile Selassie, he made his way to Kingston where he reportedly spent the next two and a half years studying the Bible to ascertain whether or not the crowning of the Ethiopian monarch was indeed the second coming of Christ. Finding that the titles 'Lion of the Tribe of Judah', 'King of Kings', and 'Lord of Lords' used for the Christ figure in Revelations 2:5 and 19:16 corresponded to those of Haile Selassie, Dunkley became convinced that he was indeed the messiah, and he started disseminating the message of Ras Tafari's divinity.

Hinds' initial black consciousness came from his exposure to Garvey's ideas and his membership in the church of Alexander Bedward, a charismatic preacher who called for the overthrow of British colonial rule in Jamaica. Convinced of Haile Selassie's divinity and liberating mission for African peoples, he joined forces with Howell, becoming his lieutenant.

All these founding Rastas had long careers and significant influence on the formation and growth of Rastafari, though Howell garnered the most public and, subsequently, academic, attention.

government moved early to forestall what it perceived as an incipient uprising. Howell and Hinds were arrested, convicted, and sent to prison on charges of sedition in 1934—Howell for two years and Hinds for one. On his release from prison Hinds founded the King of Kings Mission and successfully built a following, sometimes numbering as many as 800, but internal conflicts and power struggles eventually precipitated the demise of the group. Hinds died alone and unmourned in 1950. After his release, Howell named his group the Ethiopian Salvation Society and, by 1940, had organized a quasi commune on a somewhat remote promontory called Pinnacle in the parish of St. Catherine.

At Pinnacle, Howell was an indisputably charismatic leader. He combined the roles of prophet/preacher/teacher, autocratic administrator, legislator, judge, and folk healer. Though he appointed several assistants, they tended to exercise very little power except under his direction. Members of the community, estimates of which vary in number between 500 and 2,000, sustained themselves by working on plots apportioned to them by Howell, and families lived together in small huts. In addition to cultivating their plots, community members were required to contribute their labour to projects for the good of the community as a whole. They raised animals and grew such food crops as peas, corn, beans, and various tubers that were characteristically produced by Jamaican peasants. Their most famous crop was ganja (marijuana) which was their main cash crop sold outside the community. Though basically self-sufficient, the community maintained relationships with those on the outside. Some items such as bread were purchased from outsiders, and after children finished their pre-school education provided by the community, they continued their education at a nearby government school. Many Rastas not living at Pinnacle seemed to have made frequent visits to the community, especially for celebrations marking the coronation of His Imperial Majesty, Haile Selassie I. Music was an integral part of these celebrations, as well other community ceremonies, including a weekly Sunday afternoon drumming, singing, and dancing session. The drumming was adopted from Kumina, a spirit-possession sect that still flourishes in St. Thomas.

Retreating from his early street preaching with his haranguing of the Jamaican authorities to the tranquility of a secluded community may have been Howell's way of escaping the public gaze and official ire. However, if peace and refuge from persecution were what Howell desired, they eluded him. First of all the 'secrecy' of Howell's operation at Pinnacle bred suspicion and led to rumours that Howell was training his followers in guerilla tactics for a future assault on the Jamaican government. Additionally, when they discovered that the ganja flooding Kingston's inner city was coming from Howell's settlement, the authorities had to find a way to stem the flow. Finally, as relationships with the communities on the periphery of Pinnacle deteriorated—the peasants in these communities filed complaints alleging harassment by Howell's followers—Pinnacle came under direct police surveillance and was subjected to police raids. In 1941, the police swooped down, arresting Howell and many of his followers. Howell was imprisoned for two years, after which he returned to Pinnacle. On his return, he instituted greater security, employing the fearsome 'guardsmen' and trained dogs to patrol the perimeters of the commune. The approach of strangers was signaled by the blowing of a bull horn called a gong. Despite these measures, the police raided the commune again in 1954. This time, they destroyed all the buildings and scattered all the settlers, most of whom moved to the slums of West Kingston. Though all charges brought against Howell were later dropped, he was diagnosed as insane and committed to a mental hospital. Following the demolition of Pinnacle, Howell ceased to be the focal point of the Rastafari movement. After leaving the insane asylum, he lived with a remnant of his followers in St. Catherine until his passing in 1981.

Radical youths

Even before the demise of Pinnacle, a new aggregation of young Rastas was already charting a more radical and distinctive course than the founding elders. While the early Rastas decried the Jamaican colonial government and espoused repatriation for the black population, they operated within the religious folk ethos dominated by Revivalism. For example, early Rastafarian leaders followed the Revivalists in marching their followers to rivers for water baptism, holding street meetings to propagate their new-found message, and performing folk healing through the use of herbs and the manipulation of spiritual forces. These Rastas were also not averse to supporting local political movements seeking mass participation in Jamaica's political process. Hinds, for example, was a strong supporter of Alexander Bustamante, a campaigner for internal self-government and workers' rights, who had founded the Jamaica Labour Party (JLP) and the Bustamante Industrial Trade Union to pursue those goals. Even the communitarian-minded followers of Howell seemed to have participated in local elections, voting for the People's National Party founded by Norman Manley to oppose the more conservative JLP. But the 1940s and 1950s saw the rise of a more militant brand of Rastafari determined to cultivate a distinctive identity for the movement.

The vanguard of this increased radicalism was a group of young Rastas known as the House of Youth Black Faith (HYBF). These Rastas lived mostly in West Kingston, in communities with names such as Back-O-Wall, Trench Town, Ackee Walk, and Dungle. Others lived in the rugged terrain of Wareika Hills, east of the city of Kingston. At the forefront of HYBF were such men as Brother Arthur, Brother Panhandle, Brother Pete, Brother Taf, and Brother Wato (Watson). Wato, who later changed his name to Ras Boanerges, seemed to have been the most influential, eventually emerging as a venerable elder among the group of Rastas known as the House of Nyabinghi. Later in his life, Wato became a travelling elder, visiting nascent Rastafarian groups in various countries to ground them in the principles and practices of Rastafari.

HYBF was determined to purge the movement of such Revival influences as the meddling with spirits, the use of holy water and candles in rituals, and the manipulation of various substances in healing rites. HYBF viewed such practices as smacking of superstition and dabbling in sorcery, and pushed for them to be discontinued. In time, even water baptism as a ritual induction into Rastafari ceased. Of course, given the independent nature of circles of Rastas, or even individual Rastas, the purge was never complete. Reports continue to surface of Rastas who are known for their mystical interaction with spiritual forces. Even reggae icon Bob Marley had a reputation for clairvoyance and the ability to channel spiritual powers. Consonant with its rejection of Revivalism, HYBF adopted a stance of non-participation in local politics. In fact, politics was renamed 'polytricks', because they regarded it as the used of trickery or crafty scheming by public officials to gain and maintain power and privilege, mostly at the expense of the poor.

More significant than the rejection of Revivalism and the refusal to participate in local politics was the HYBF's role in routinizing the salient elements of Rastafari that have since become recognizable markers of Rastafarian identity. The radical individualism that militates against the rise of centralized authority figures in the movement was cemented by the refusal of the HYBF cohorts to submit to the autocratic tendencies of men such as Howell and Hibbert. While ganja smoking was always widespread among Rastas, and for that matter the lower strata of Jamaican society from which most Rastas came, it was elevated to the status of sacred ritual by the militant youths of the 1940s and 1950s. Going beyond the prodigious growth of hair on both their heads and faces that was cultivated by some of their elders, the youth of HYBF started allowing their hair to grow naturally without being disturbed by scissors and combs, producing long, matted tresses of 'dreadlocks' that came to symbolize the strength and courage of Rastas. These elements of Rastafari will be explored in a later chapter.

The militancy of the youthful Rastas of the 1940s and 1950s was met by a determined campaign by the Jamaican authorities to repress the movement. This militancy was expressed by groups of Rastas marching through Kingston, holding public meetings in which they harangued the oppressive social system, and staging a symbolic capture of public property such as Victoria Park in the central square of downtown Kingston and Kings House, the residence of the governor general. With their smoking of ganja, they defied the dangerous substance laws of 1930 and 1941, and when brought to court for infraction of these laws, they refused to follow the code of conduct deemed appropriate for legal proceedings. For example, they often refused to swear on the Bible or offer a plea, and frequently spewed condemnation at judges, attorneys, and other court officials. Their unconventional hairstyles and their inscrutable language placed them outside the boundaries of social acceptability in Jamaica. Some even refused to work in a system based on the exploitation of the labour of the many by a few. Preachers, politicians, journalists, and ordinary people ascribed to them laziness, lunacy, and criminality as endemic traits. What is more, the authorities viewed their anti-government sentiments as disposing them to manipulation by communists and other radicals bent on overthrowing the legally constituted government. Rastafari thus became subjected to a systemic campaign of repression by Jamaican authorities. Their meetings were treated as a public nuisance and frequently broken up by the police. Violent acts or public disturbances in the inner city areas were summarily attributed to Rastas, giving the police unchecked authority to carry out indiscriminate searches, harassment, and arrest of members of the movement. For the slightest provocation, and even without provocation, policed often subjected Rastas to beatings or the shearing of their locks.

Repatriation fever

An escalation of the conflict between Rastas and the Jamaican authorities took place in the context of a repatriation fever that began sweeping the movement towards the end of the 1950s. Contributing to this heightened aspiration for a return to Africa were undoubtedly the creation of the State of Israel in 1948 as the homeland of diasporic Jews from around the world, the wave of Jamaicans emigrating to England and North America after World War II, and a 1955 communiqué from the Ethiopia World Federation (EWF) informing Local 31 in Jamaica of a 500-acre land grant by Haile Selassie to blacks in the Americas who wished to migrate to Ethiopia.

Two prominent figures of the Rastafari movement raised the expectation for repatriation even higher in 1958 and 1959. Prince Emmanuel Edwards called an assembly of Rastas in 1958 and attracted an estimated 3,000 followers from around the country. Many seemed to have viewed the gathering as a precursor of or preparation for leaving for the motherland of Africa. Thus many disposed of whatever possessions they had in anticipation of their departure. The main activities of this gathering were nightly drumming, dancing, and 'speechifying' against the evils of Jamaican society. Towards the end of the assembly, many Rastas marched to Victoria Park staging a symbolic capture. For this they incurred the ire of Jamaican police who moved in to dislodge them. The very next year, Claudius Henry, the self-styled 'Repairer of the Breach' and 'Moses of the Blacks,' invited Rastas and others desirous of returning to Africa to visit his headquarters in preparation for departure to Africa. The invitation card, a reported 15,000 copies of which were sold for one shilling each (about ten cents), clearly stated that the holder was being invited to an 'Emancipation Jubilee' and that it was to be retained as a kind of travel document. Thousands descended on Kingston with their belongings amidst rumours that ships were waiting in the Kingston harbour to provide them with passage to Africa. When the appointed day came and went with no sign of the vessels to transport them, disappointment and disbelief descended on those gathered. Some drifted back to their places of abode; others lingered around Henry's premises for a while because they had sold their properties in expectation of repatriation. Henry was eventually arrested and charged with disturbing the peace. He was released on probation and given a fine of £100. The stir that he created and his subsequent vitriol against the Jamaican government brought Henry under police surveillance. When it was reported to the police that he was plotting an uprising, they raided his premises and found a stash of weapons including a shotgun, a revolver, numerous machetes with both sides sharpened, a large collection of detonators, and some explosives. Henry was convicted of treason and sentenced to prison for six years.

Not long after Henry's incarceration, a guerilla cell led by his son, Ronald, was reportedly training in the Red Hills north of Kingston in preparation for an assault on the government. The group included some African-American colleagues of Ronald Henry and a number of Rastas whom they had recruited. When a combined police and military force, including British soldiers, went to investigate, two of the soldiers were gunned down in an ambush. When the assailants were later tracked down and apprehended, the bodies of three Rastafarian men were also discovered. They were reportedly executed for leaking information about the group. Ronald Henry and his African-American colleagues were convicted and executed for insurrection and murder. This incident confirmed in the minds of the authorities and Jamaican public what they had long feared and argued, that Rastas harboured a disposition for violence that was often intensified by ganja smoking.

The collective hysteria that gripped Jamaica in the wake of the Henrys affair fueled an escalation of repression against Rastafari. Rastas were no longer regarded as curious misfits or belonging to a lunatic fringe. Many people seriously believed that they were a credible threat to national security, and they were treated that way by politicians and law enforcement. The then premier, Norman Manley, used the country's newspapers to castigate the Rastas as dangerous enemies of Jamaica and a serious threat to its push for independence. He appealed to the public to monitor and report on the movements and activities of Rastas.

Tentative rapprochement

The pressure on the Rastafari movement was so great that Mortimer Planno, a leading Rasta, approached Dr Arthur Lewis, the principal of University College of the West Indies (later University of the West Indies), inviting him to send a group of social scientists to study the movement in order to educate the public about the true nature of Rastafari. With the approval of Premier Manley, Lewis dispatched M. G. Smith, Roy Augier, and Rex Nettleford, young academicians at the university, to conduct an ethnographic survey of the movement in Kingston. Though the scholars spent only two weeks conducting this study, they produced a report ('Report on the Rastafari Movement in Kingston, Jamaica') that became a kind of public policy document that provided the impetus for a thawing in the conflictual relationship between Rastafari and the rest of Jamaican society. The study made clear that while criminal elements existed on the fringe of

the movement, and while criminals have used the cover of
Rastafari to ply their trade, Rastas in general promoted peace and
communality, as exemplified in their often heard greeting: 'peace
and love'. Though their denunciation of the status quo was often
suffused with violent language, as in their frequent invocation of
'blood and fire' on their perceived enemies, this kind of speech was
in the mode of the Hebrew prophets and was not to be understood
as incitement to use violence against constituted authority. What
is more, the study indicated that the lack of economic opportunities, amenities such as water, sewage, and roads, and social
services such health care, education and recreation faced by most
Rastas and the poor in general were social maladies that should be
addressed by the government. Furthermore, the scholars argued
that the issue of repatriation which was occupying centre stage of
the movement was not to be treated as a wild collective dream.
They recommended that the Jamaican government explore the
possibility of Jamaicans migrating to Africa as part of its broader
policy of encouraging emigration as a solution to endemic
unemployment in Jamaica.

Though the report received mixed reviews from the Jamaican
public, it marked an important watershed in the relationship
between Rastafari and the broader Jamaican society. Most
significantly, the systemic and indiscriminate persecution of
Rastas abated immediately following the study. This is not to say
the negative image of Rastafari changed completely or that police
harassment of Rastas disappeared from Jamaican society.
As ensuing events were to reveal, the association of Rastas with
criminality prevailed throughout the 1960s. In 1963 in Coral
Gardens, Montego Bay, a running squabble between developers
and Rastas who squatted in the hills above Rose Hall and used a
footpath across the Rose Hall Estate escalated into an outburst of
violence that resulted in a confrontation with police, causing
several deaths, many arrests, and the demolition of homes and
settlements. When violence and criminality in Back O'Wall
reached crisis proportions in the mid 1960s, fingers were again

Coral Gardens

The violent events occurring at Coral Gardens in 1963 were
initiated when an enraged Rasta, who had been beaten by police
during an altercation with an attendant at a nearby petrol station,
conspired with a few fellow Rastas to burn the station down. This
triggered a series of events leading to the deaths of several
people. The police and members of the military not only tracked
down the offending Rastas, but unleashed a new round of official
violence against Rastas in the Montego Bay area. Alexander
Bustamante, the prime minister, reportedly issued an order to
'bring them in dead or alive'. No official numbers were released,
but Rasta eyewitnesses claimed that hundreds were killed by the
security forces; many more were arrested and jailed; homes and
settlements were demolished; and those wishing to escape the
onslaught had to flee to the hills, relocate to other parts of the
country, or cut their locks and shave their beards to avoid the ire
of the police. Rastas in Montego Bay still commemorate the event
of Coral Gardens as a reminder of the repressive measures taken
against them.

pointed at Rastafari. In response, the government sent in heavy
equipment that completely razed the shacks of the squatters,
including many Rastas.

Despite the incidents of official repression, the 1960s brought more
favourable winds as Rastas sailed the turbulent waters of what they
considered an alien culture. In response to a recommendation in
the 'Report on the Rastafari Movement in Kingston, Jamaica', the
government of Norman Manley sent a delegation to Africa in 1961
to investigate the possibility of repatriation. The envoys included
three Rastas: Mortimer Planno, Filmore Alvaranga, and Douglas
Mack. The official report of the mission to Nigeria, Ghana, Liberia,
Sierra Leone and Ethiopia noted that the Jamaicans were received
warmly and that the governments of these countries were generally

4. Rasta women marking the anniversary of the Coral Gardens Incident, Montego Bay, 1999

well disposed to the idea of the descendants of enslaved Africans eventually returning to the continent. However, they were only interested in receiving educated and skilled repatriates who could assist in the development process. The Rastas on the mission authored their own report that portrayed African governments waiting to receive them unreservedly. Unfortunately, repatriation was pursued no further at an official level. The Rastafarian delegates organized a second mission in 1963, but without the official support of the Jamaican government, they encountered many financial and diplomatic difficulties.

The Jamaican government's policy of developing relationships with African nations and inviting a parade of African dignitaries to visit Jamaica can be construed as another gesture of accommodation to Rastas. Some scholars argue that this effort was to acknowledge and celebrate the historical and cultural links between Jamaica and Africa. Others contend that it was a carefully calibrated effort to expose Rastas to the realities of Africa and discourage them from wanting to repatriate. The most significant visit was that of Haile Selassie, who made an official visit to Jamaica in 1966. Commentators still assert that no other visitor to Jamaica before or since has come close to creating the kind of excitement that Selassie did. Among the mass of people who blanketed the airport were thousands of Rastas who came to get a glimpse of the one they considered the divine liberator of African peoples. They descended on the airport in their clothing and accessories of red, green, and gold; broke through the barrier surrounding the tarmac, and surrounded the emperor's plane when it arrived. The efforts of the Jamaican officials and the security forces failed to push back the crowds so the emperor could disembark. Only the appeal of Mortimer Planno prevailed upon the crowd to pull back from the tarmac to allow Selassie to deplane. Rastas still tell tales of marvellous happenings during Selassie's visit. For example, just before the emperor's plane arrived on what had been a rainy and cloudy day, a white dove appeared from the clouds, and immediately the clouds lifted, the sun came out, and the emperor's plane came into view. Rita Marley, Bob Marley's wife, reported becoming convinced that Selassie was the reincarnated Christ when, as he passed by, he looked her in the eyes and waved his hands revealing the scars of the nails with which he had been fixed to the cross during his crucifixion. The rising status of Rastas was evident in their invitations to attend official functions at a fancy hotel and at Kings House, the official residence of the governor general. Rastas also requested, and were granted, a private audience with the African monarch.

Detractors of Rastafari were hoping that the emperor would put to rest the 'heretic' assertion of Rastas that he was God. Some thought that his public assertion that he was only a man and a devoted Christian was enough to settle the question. However, Rastas emerged from their private conference with him insisting that he had confided to them that 'I am He.' Additionally, they claimed he instructed them to remain in Jamaica to work for the liberation of its black people before repatriating to Africa. In the period immediately following the emperor's visit, the phrase 'liberation before repatriation' came into vogue in some segments of the movement. Accordingly, activism around the issue of repatriation declined significantly.

Sympathetic embrace

By the late 1960s, elements of the Rastafarian ethos were penetrating the consciousness of Jamaican youths. Both poor urban and rural youths were walking like Rastas, wearing Rastafarian accessories in the signature red, green, and gold, adopting elements of Dreadtalk (Rastafarian argot), and spouting elements of Rastafarian philosophy, especially when talking about the corruption and inefficiency of the upper classes and the government. 'Rasta-minded' and 'Rasta sympathizers' became designations for those youths showing any affinity for Rastafari. In time, many of them embraced the movement fully. Particularly disturbing for the middle class guardians of the status quo was the conversion of middle class youths to Rastafari. Many of these new adherents found a home in the emerging group of Rastas known as the Twelve Tribes of Israel. Often dubbed 'Uptown Rastas', Twelve Tribes came to be associated with the educated, the musicians, and the artists who embraced Rastafari. With the spread of Black Power philosophy and activism among the rising

A measure of respectability for Rastafari

The international success of reggae with such artists as Bob Marley and the Wailers led to its celebration (as the epitome of local culture) by Jamaicans of all classes and to the 'lionization' of these artists as creators and purveyors of Jamaica's popular culture. The elevated regard for Rastafari was demonstrated in 1976 and 1978 when political violence in Kingston between rival inner city communities threatened to erupt. Instead of summarily blaming and arresting Rastas, leading politicians approached Rastafarian leaders and musicians for their assistance in defusing the volatile situation. The 'Smile Jamaica' concert in 1976 and the 'Peace Concert' of 1978, both headlined by Bob Marley, cast Rastas in the role of peace makers. The awarding of the Order of Merit to Bob Marley by the Jamaican government on 20 April 1981 and the state funeral he was accorded after his death less than a month later clearly demonstrated that Rastafari had come in from the cold (to use Marley's image) of marginalization to the shelter of respectability.

educated class in the Caribbean, young black power advocates came to appreciate the anti-establishment stance which the Rastas had maintained for almost forty years. These legitimated Rastafarian critiques, of Jamaican and Western society by forming alliances with members of the movement, as exemplified by the Black Power activist and university lecturer, Walter Rodney, who spent much time teaching African history to Rastas and reasoning with them about politics and culture. Others fully embraced Rastafari, as did Cat Coore, son of David Coore, a former finance minister and deputy prime minister. An important factor in Rastafari's penetration of the consciousness of the poor and its validation by the educated youth was the emergence of reggae with strains of the Rastafari drumming in the music and the suffusion of the lyrics with the Rastafarian outlook.

The 1970s were characterized by a remarkable shift in the influence of Rastafari on broader social processes in Jamaica. One demonstration of this shift was the dramatic and theatric manipulation of Rastafarian sensibilities and religious symbols in election campaigns during this decade. In these campaigns, Michael Manley and the People's National Party (PNP), and to a lesser extent the Jamaica Labour Party (JLP) employed and deployed reggae, Rastafarian language, and Rastafarian symbols to appeal to the masses among whom Rastafarian sensibilities had become diffused by the early 1970s. Nothing exemplifies this more than Manley's use of a walking stick that he dubbed the rod of correction. Supposedly acquired as a gift from Emperor Haile Selassie I on a visit to Ethiopia and interpreted through the lens of Rastafari, the rod became a symbol of Manley's divine mission to correct the wrongs of Jamaican society. Assuming the persona of a deliverer by taking the biblical name Joshua (Moses' lieutenant who led the Hebrews across the Jordan into the promised land of Canaan), Manley travelled across Jamaica brandishing his rod and employing reggae music, Rastafarian symbols, and street language to promise change for the 'sufferahs' with the slogan 'Better Must Come' from Delroy Wilson's song. At the same time, he excoriated the JLP by declaring 'Dem haffi get a beatin' ('They have to get a beating') in the words of Peter Tosh's song of the same name. Using this approach, Manley and the PNP won the general election in 1972 and again in 1976. This kind of manipulation of Rastafari by the mainstream may have been self-serving and disingenuous, however, it moved Rastafari from the despised margins to the centre of political discourse and thereby conferred a measure of legitimacy on the Rastafarian cause.

Ebbing militancy

While Rastafari exerted a positive force on Jamaican society during the 1970s when it was considered the creative edge of Jamaican popular culture, the 1980s and beyond have been characterized by an ebbing of the vitality of the Rastafarian presence in society. Several forces were at work leading to the downturn in Rastafarian public influence. To begin with, many Rastas felt exploited by the politicians of the 1970s who used their language and symbols to appeal to the voting public without doing anything concrete to help their cause. In a similar vein, the rhetoric of socialism and Afrocentrism by Michael Manley had raised hopes that the poor would experience social and economic justice in Jamaica, but the coming to power of Edward Seaga of the JLP in 1980 on a pro-western, pro-capitalism platform dashed those hopes, and Rastas retreated somewhat from the public square. The gnawing reality of the death of Haile Selassie in 1975 and Bob Marley in 1981 must have dampened the enthusiasm of some Rastas and lessened the attraction of Rastafari for the youth. That Selassie and Rastas could not die had been a long-held belief in Rastafari. Death was seen as 'the wages of sin' for those who were not conscious of their divine selves and who contravened the principles of righteous living. Since Selassie was God incarnate and Rastas were living according to the righteous principles of Jah (God), they were assured 'everliving life'. More conservative Rastas asserted that Marley's death was the result of his sin of becoming enmeshed with the corrupt, exploitative corporate music industry of Babylon. These lines of argument notwithstanding, the passing of these and other notable figures in Rastafari placed Rastas on the defensive. Rastas have since tried to come to terms with the reality of death with the passing of more and more first and second generation Rastas. They have adopted the term 'transition' to indicate that those who die are leaving time and space and moving into another realm of existence. Importantly, some Rastafarian elders are reportedly developing funerary rituals to mark the transitioning of Rastas.

The most conspicuous area of the declining influence of Rastafari was in Jamaica's popular music (Reggae and its significance will be discussed more fully in Chapter 6). In hindsight, the death of Bob Marley seems more than just the passing of Jamaica's most acclaimed superstar. It marked the transition from the Rasta-inspired, socially conscious lyrics that suffused the vintage reggae of the 1970s, to the male braggadocio, sexual explicit 'slackness,' and gratuitous celebration of gun violence of dancehall (deejay, ragga) music that has dominated the Jamaican airwaves since the 1980s.

After 1980, most young people showing interest in spiritual matters turned instead to Pentecostal and Charismatic groups with lively liturgies that often employed local musical forms, including reggae. That trajectory continued with the conversion of some Rastas to evangelical Christianity, especially since the mid-1990s. The conversion of prominent Rastas such as Judith Mowatt, solo artist as well as backing singer of Bob Marley, and Tommy Cowan, legendary reggae producer, promoter, and MC, received much publicity in Jamaica and beyond. These ex-Rastas did not just withdraw from their former allegiance to occupy quietly the pews of a church. Though they have not become virulently anti-Rasta, they have embarked on active and public Christian ministries in which they are utilizing their musical talents in general and reggae in particularly. What is more, both Mowatt and Cowan have insisted that during his last days, Marley converted to Christianity as was evidenced in his baptism in the

Rastafarian images as tourist wares

One area in which the influence of Rastafari has remained ubiquitous since the 1980s is the 'cultural' art and crafts that fill markets and roadside stalls in places frequented by tourists. Multitudes of carvings and drawings of Rastafarian images and the prolific use of Rastafarian colours on t-shirts, hats, scarves, and jewellry greet potential buyers at these sites. But here, neither Rastafarian spirituality nor Rastafarian social and cultural ideals are being advanced. Instead, commercial impulses have made the Rastafarian image and symbols into commodities to satisfy the tourists' hankering after the exotic.

Ethiopian Orthodox Church. Such conversions and assertions about the most famous Rasta have angered some adherents of Rastafari who have responded with characteristically militant rhetoric captured in the phrase, 'bun Jeezas' (Burn Jesus), to express their disdain for the converts and their declarations.

Although the energy and enthusiasm that Rastafari generated in the 1960s and 1970s have subsided somewhat since the 1980s, Rastafari has remained a significant presence in Jamaican society. Furthermore, as Rastafari spread abroad, a number of leading Rastas have invested their energies in building up Rastafarian communities outside Jamaica and in shaping Rastafari's international identity through missions, conferences, and workshops. Since the mid-1990s, a new cohort of Rastafarian reggae musicians have emerged on Jamaica's music scene with the express purpose of expunging 'slackness' and returning Rastafarian spirituality and social consciousness to a central place in reggae. Though the bawdy, salacious, and violence-laced lyrics continue to characterize the dancehall genre, such artists as Anthony B, Luciano, Sizzla, Capleton, and Buju Banton now provide a counterweight with their Rastafarian spirituality, social criticism, and positive cultural vibes.

Stirrings of a desire to be involved in the political process have also become evident among some Rastas. Even though the dominant strain in Rastafari has been to eschew any involvement in politics, since the 1990s new voices have called for the organization of Rastafari into a political force in Jamaica and elsewhere. In fact, as early as 1985, Rastafarian scholar and public intellectual Leachim Semaj had called for Rastafari to move beyond being a religious and cultural force in Jamaica to becoming the shaper of social and political institutions. More recently, younger and more educated Rastas have called for the centralization of the movement to create a united front that can advocate and agitate for the rights and causes of Rastas. One such cause is the legalization of ganja, for which Rastas have joined other progressive forces in a campaign since the 1990s. In recent general elections in Jamaica a number of Rastas have contested parliamentary seats. This was initiated by Ras Astor Black who formed the Jamaican Alliance Movement in 2002 and furthered by the Imperial Ethiopian World Federation Incorporated Political Party (IEWFIPP), formed by the Church of Haile Selassie. In 2007, a total of nine Rastas were on the ballots. So far, they have garnered only minimal support from the electorate.

During my visit to Jamaica in January 2011, I found Rastas ensconced at all levels of Jamaican society. I encountered them selling foodstuffs in the public markets and on the roadsides, hawking their wares in craft markets, and working on road crews. I observed that they make frequent appearances on radio and television as presenters and guests. I lunched and conversed with at least two Rastafarian colleagues who are lecturers at the University of the West Indies, and I am acquainted with two others who are on the faculty there. As is to be expected, Rastas are duly represented in music and the visual arts (discussed more fully in Chapter 6).

Chapter 2
'Rastalogy' and 'livity': the principles and practices of Rastafari

Though Rastafari has no professional clergy or theologians, it has developed a fairly cohesive worldview, adopted an evocative array of symbols, and assumed a distinctive lifestyle. Rastas and scholars of Rastafari employ the term 'Rastalogy' to designate the totality of Rastafarian ideas, and 'livity' to characterize the cultural and religious practices of the movement. While heterogeneity of beliefs and practices pervades the ethos of Rastafari, adherents of the movement embrace the centrality of Haile Selassie, the importance of InI consciousness, the critique of Babylon and aspiration for repatriation, the iconic dreadlocks and consciousness-raising 'dreadtalk', and the pursuit of livity.

Selassie I and InI

From its very inception, Rastafari has been inextricably linked to Haile Selassie I. The very name of the movement is derived from Ras (a title meaning duke or prince) and Tafari Makonen, the pre-regnal name of Emperor Haile Selassie I. His crowning in November 1930 (see Figure 4) as Haile Selassie I ('power of the trinity') and his honorific titles, 'King of Kings, Lord of Lords, Conquering Lion of the Tribe of Judah, and Elect of God', fired the imagination of some Jamaicans who had adopted biblical messianism and merged it with the hope of black liberation. Many became convinced, after personal reflection and study of the Bible,

5. Coronation of Haile Selassie with his wife Empress Menen

that Haile Selassie I was the messianic figure prophesied in the
Bible and the black liberator that many had hoped would emerge
to restore Africa and Africans, whether in the homeland or the

diaspora, to their former glory. Hence, in the years following Haile Selassie's elevation to emperor of Ethiopia, several preachers appeared on street corners in Jamaica proclaiming that he was Christ in his second coming, in which he had been reborn as a black, kingly figure destined to end European expansionism and exploitation and bring peace and justice to the oppressed of the world — especially African peoples.

While the above understanding of Selassie's place in Rastafari seems straightforward enough and while most Rastas accord him a place of prominence and esteem, they differ in their understanding of his essential nature and identity. Rastas belonging to the Nyabinghi Order, which holds tenaciously to the most traditional ethos of Rastafari, insist that to be an authentic Rasta a person must affirm that Ras Tafari (Haile Selassie I) was/is a divine manifestation in human form. This, they contend, is the irreducible core of Rastafari. However, even within the Nyabinghi Order Rastas have proffered a variety of opinions regarding Selassie's relationship to the Supreme Being. For some, he is Jah Rastafari, the almighty creator appearing in human form. Others reserve the designation Jah (short for Jehovah or Yahweh) for the eternal, supreme ruler of the universe, while identifying Selassie as the messianic figure of the Hebrew Bible and the Christ figure of the New Testament. In this view, Selassie is a divine messenger sent to accomplish Jah's will on earth. Some Rastas, notably the dub poet Mutabaruka, assert that God is not an ethereal supernatural or metaphysical entity existing outside the world,

Haile Selassie: a bio

Tafari Makonnen I was born on 23 July 1892 to Ras Makonnen Wolde Mikael Guddisa (who was a first cousin to Menelik II, the reigning monarch, and who had been appointed governor of the Ethiopian province of Harar in 1887) and Yeshimebet Ali. In 1916, Tafari became regent of Ethiopia and was accorded the title Ras (head, duke, or prince). As regent, he ruled Ethiopia along with Empress Zaudita until her passing in 1930. Elevated to emperor, Ras Tafari took the name Haile Selassie ('Power of the Trinity'), probably to reflect his new status as head of the Ethiopian Orthodox Church. He also took the title 'Conquering Lion of the Tribe of Judah, King of Kings of Ethiopia, Elect of God' affirming the legend of the *Kebra Negast* ('Glory of Kings') that traces the genealogy of the Ethiopian royal family to Menelik I, who was reportedly born to King Solomon of Israel and the Queen of Sheba (Queen Makeda) in the mid-900s BCE. The Italian invasion of Ethiopia in 1935 forced Haile Selassie into exile in London, from where he led the resistance until the Italians were defeated in 1941.

Selassie's major national accomplishment was the modernization of Ethiopia, moving it out of the feudalism that had prevailed well into the first half of the 1900s. This included the modernization of schools and law enforcement agencies, and the adoption of a new constitution, which, while preserving the power of the nobility, was nonetheless viewed as a precursor to democracy. Regionally, Selassie became a leading voice against European colonialism in Africa and a supporter of the Independence movement that led to the independence of most African nations, beginning with Ghana in 1957. Internationally, Selassie used the League of Nations (which Ethiopia joined in 1936) and the United Nations to campaign for international peace and human rights and against the proliferation of weapons of mass destruction.

Faced with a secessionist uprising in Eritrea and weakened by the poor economic condition of Ethiopia, which was exacerbated by a deadly famine in the early 1970s, the ageing Selassie was deposed in a coup d'état led by Mengitsu Haile Mariam in 1974. The next year, Selassie, who had been confined to his palace, was declared dead under suspicious circumstances. His remains were found buried under a palace toilet in 1992, and later interred in the Holy Trinity Cathedral in Addis Ababa.

but a consciousness of the self as divine. This is in keeping with the often repeated aphorism of Rastafari, 'God is man and man is God'. From this perspective, Selassie is not a *supernatural* being but the *supreme* man because he has fully realized his divine selfhood, and this qualifies him as 'earth's rightful ruler'. This understanding of the divine probably informs the divine trinity of Haile Selassie, Marcus Garvey, and Prince Emmanuel Edwards, as propounded by the Rastafarian group called the Bobo Dreads, Bobo Shanti, or more formally Ethiopia Africa Black International Congress (EABIC).

While holding Haile Selassie in high esteem, the Twelve Tribes of Israel, commonly regarded as the most liberal and 'Christian' of all Rastafarian groups, focuses mainly on Jesus Christ of the New Testament as the redemptive hope for humankind. Referred to as Yahshua or Yesus Kritos, Jesus Christ will return to earth in a second coming to consummate the salvific process he began at his first coming. Haile Selassie is/was not that second coming; rather, he is God's vessel of the modern age, chosen to perpetuate the Davidic kingdom, which God himself promised would last forever. Like the Twelve Tribes of Israel, a growing group that calls itself Fulfilled Rastafari looks to Yahshua as savior and regards Selassie as his messenger in this era. Hence, Selassie's life and his teachings as expressed in his writings and speeches are studied for guidance and inspiration. Both the Twelve Tribes and the Fulfilled Rastafari put great emphasis on Selassie's struggle against colonialism in Africa and for the independence of African nations; his campaign for African unity and his role in founding the Organization of African Unity (which later became the African Union); his speeches to the League of Nations and United Nations calling for world peace and the end of the build-up of armament capable of exterminating humankind; and his frequent calls for human rights, respect for human dignity, and tolerance among people of all ethnicities, cultures, and religion.

When Marxist revolutionaries overthrew the Ethiopian monarchy in 1975, the resultant murder of Haile Selassie I constituted a potential crisis of faith for the many Rastas who had previously acclaimed him as God or divine in some respect, and as such not subject to death. However, a variety of responses emanating from Rastas effectively forestalled any such crisis. Refusing to accept the reports of Selassie's death, Rastafari apologists castigated the media as Western propaganda machines disseminating misinformation, and they supported this contention by pointing to the fact that no body had been produced and no interment site identified (as mentioned earlier, the body had been buried secretly under a toilet in the Imperial Palace and was not found until 1992, after which it was interred in Trinity Cathedral in Addis Ababa in November 2000).

Those who did accept the physical passing of Selassie argued that the man had just been the bodily carriage for the eternal being, the death of the body was to be expected and was therefore of little importance, for the eternal spirit lives on. Faced with derision over the death of their 'god', others followed Bob Marley in rising above the din of ridicule and simply asserting 'Fools sayin' in their heart, Rasta your God is dead. Jah live! Children yeah!' ('Jah Lives').

For many Rastas, the 'I' after Selassie is multivalent in its significance. Read as 'first', it points to his pre-existence from the beginning and to his preeminence as earth's 'rightful ruler'. Read as the first person singular pronoun 'I', which is generally how Rastas pronounce it, it becomes an indicator of Selassie's divinity. From this understanding, Rastas extrapolate that 'I' represents the divine essence of humans. They then elaborated the philosophy of InI consciousness ('Isciousness') as the realization of one's own divine identity. To an outsider, attaching such meaning to a seemingly minute detail may appear ludicrous, but for Rastas it is a plucky act of asserting a positive identity and affirming the wholesome dignity and creative agency of their black selves. For members of a group whose self-worth had been immolated on the altar of profit-making during the colonial enterprise, and whose marginalized existence in the underside of Jamaican society had been criminalized, the profession of InI consciousness repudiates all negative perceptions of their African past, their underclass status in Jamaican society, and their subjugation to the capitalist world order. The linguistic twist in the use of the first person I also indicates Rastas' determination to be active subjects in fashioning their identity and terms of engagement with the world. As Bob Marley sang, 'We refuse to be what you wanted us to be; we are what we are; and that's the way it's going to be' ('Babylon System'). Though it was initially meant to elevate the black underclass from which the early Rastas came, the idea that 'I' represents the core of the divine that resides in all human beings lends universality to the InI philosophy. If consciousness of this divine essence is what makes a person Rastafari, then persons of all races can 'sight up' (come to embrace) Rastafari by becoming enlightened to the divine within.

From Babylon to Zion

That Haile Selassie I is a redeeming messianic figure implies that those to be delivered are in some kind of bondage and exile. That sense of bondage and exile is captured in the word 'Babylon'. Rastas adopted this term from the ancient biblical city of Babylon in Mesopotamia, which built an empire that dominated the Middle East in the seventh and sixth centuries BCE. Among Babylon's victims were the Jews, whose capital city and temple were looted and levelled and whose people were taken into exile in a series of deportations between 597 and 586 BCE. In the New Testament, the Book of Revelation features the term 'Babylon' as a code word for the Roman Empire. To Christians facing persecution from Roman authorities, the Empire that exploited the poor and persecuted the righteous approximated the spirit of ancient Babylon.

Rastas, who regard themselves as either the descendants or reincarnations of the ancient Hebrews, find the Babylonian spirit present in the modern world. Colonialism, which thrived on territorial expansion and the exploitation of forced labour in the

Polytricks

Rastas were not always averse to supporting local political movements seeking mass participation in Jamaica's political process. Though Rastas decried the existing colonial government in Jamaica, Robert Hinds, for example, was a strong supporter of Alexander Bustamante, a campaigner for internal self-government and workers' rights and founder of the Jamaica Labour Party (JLP) and the Bustamante Industrial Trade Union which pursued those goals. In the first Jamaican election held with universal adult suffrage in 1944, Hinds encouraged his followers to vote for the JLP. Leonard P. Howell was an admirer of Norman Manley and voted for the People's National Party (PNP), which Manley had founded. But the 1940s and 1950s saw the rise of a more militant group of Rastas who branded politics as 'polytricks'—deceptive schemes of the upper classes to gain and maintain power and privilege. The phenomenon of political 'tribalism' that has become a feature of Jamaican politics since the 1960s has not only confirmed the Rastafarian belief that politicians are deceptive, but has also demonstrated that their methods are divisive. The trademark of political tribalism is the provision of guns and patronage to young men in inner city communities in return for intimidating community members to vote for their patrons. As the two main parties (JLP and PNP) armed different communities, conflicts or 'tribal wars' became endemic among Kingston inner city communities. Bob Marley captures this aspect of polytricks in 'Ambush in the Night'. He describes how those fighting for power use guns and money to bribe young people and to divide them into competing camps that fight and kill one another for meagre hand-outs.

Americas and elsewhere, thus becomes a more recent iteration of Babylon. Global capitalism, which extracts resources from less developed countries, exploits the labour of the working class, and disproportionately enriches those individuals and countries that control capital, constitutes a contemporary manifestation of

Babylon. Social, political, and economic institutions which funnel power and privilege to a few, are also expressions of this Babylonian spirit, and soldiers and police who protect the power and privilege of the few and enforce the laws that guarantee inequity are agents of Babylon. To use Bob Marley's stinging words, they are 'all dressed in uniforms of brutality' ('Burnin and Lootin'). Thus, by this evocative term, Rastas effectively delegitimize the vaunted institutions of the Western world that have been lauded as the zenith of human social and cultural achievements.

The more personal aspect of Babylon's misdeeds for Rastafari is the forced deportation of an estimated 10 to 15 million Africans to the Americas, where they and their descendants were held in bondage and exploited as slaves from the 1500s to the 1800s, and mostly condemned to poverty ever since. Even the social and cultural systems under which they live have been designed to divest them of their African culture, heritage, and identity. Both religious and educational institutions (sometimes they were one and the same) conspire either to denigrate Africa as savage and uncivilized or to withhold knowledge of its accomplishments in human history. In the words of the Rastafarian lyricist, they are 'building church and universities, deceiving the people continually' (Bob Marley, 'Babylon System'). For Rastas, therefore, black people in the West are exiles in Babylon, alienated from their African homeland, their African culture, and their sense of African identity. The objective of Rastafari is to delegitimize and destroy, or 'chant down', Babylon, restoring black people to their African selves and their status as human beings endowed with divine consciousness.

In contrast to the Babylonian West, with its alienating and oppressive social institutions, Rastas invoke the term 'Zion' as the ideal to which they aspire. As with Babylon, Zion is adopted from the biblical corpus, where it is the designation for an idealized Jerusalem, the city of God. The word 'Jerusalem' means 'city of peace'; to the Rastas, it represents justice, harmony, and community. In Rastafari, Zion/Jerusalem is transmuted to Africa or Ethiopia. As a result, Africa seems to take on a mythological identity in the Rastafarian discourse. As with countless other cultures, the creation of myths is an ancient and modern strategy to ground the Rastas' self-understanding in a realm that is beyond falsification. The positing of Africa as Zion, the true home of Rastas and all black people, speaks to a desire to escape the domination and degradation experienced under the Babylonian system of the West.

The Babylonian condition of the West and the projection of Zionic conditions on Africa underlie the Rastas' desire for repatriation. At its inception amidst the throes of economic hardship, workers' agitation, and political activism in Jamaica in the 1930s, Rastas dismissed any hope of redemption in the West and declared their desire to return to the African homeland of their forebears. Particularly in the first 30 years of Rastafari's existence, repatriation to Africa occupied a central place in the movement. Rastas argued that since their ancestors were forcibly deported from Africa, the British colonial government, the Jamaican government since its independence in 1962, or the United Nations should undertake to return them to their homeland. To this end, Rastas have made repeated appeals to the Jamaican and British governments and to the United Nations to secure the means of repatriation. Some have had hopes for a miraculous or mysterious means of return. Early Rastafarian leaders, such as Howell and Henry, went as far as to set dates for the arrival of ships in Kingston harbour, most likely sent by Haile Selassie I, to convey Rastas to Africa. Others have resorted to more practical means of repatriation, employing their own resources and ingenuity to secure passage to Africa. The Twelve Tribes of Israel reportedly has a programme for funding, relocating, and supporting their members in Africa, which certainly accounts for the significant numbers of Twelve Tribes members who have repatriated to and are exerting considerable influence over the Shashamane Rastafarian community in

Ethiopia. However, since the emergence of the 'liberation before repatriation' message, supposedly endorsed by Haile Selassie I during his visit to Jamaica in 1966, and the increased acceptance of Rastafari into the Jamaican mainstream, the Rastafarian fervour for repatriation seem to have abated somewhat. Some have even promulgated a more psycho-cultural understanding of repatriation as the re-appropriation of African heritage and self-understanding rather than a physical return to the land of Africa. Nevertheless, the desire for literal repatriation remains high on the agenda of many Rastas and still represents the Zion ideal to many others. At a Rastafari Studies Conference at the University of the West Indies, Mona, Jamaica, in August 2010, the Rastas calling for development and execution of repatriation schemes were quite vociferous during the question and answer periods in a number of sessions.

Dreadlocks and dreadtalk

In rejecting Babylon's aesthetic of grooming and Babylon's language conventions, Rastas have developed the iconic dreadlocks hairstyle and their own argot, commonly referred to as 'dreadtalk' or 'Rasta talk' and as 'Iyaric' by others. From the very beginning of the movement, members of Rastafari were known for their full beards and tall hair. This practice may have been an attempt to imitate the facial hair of Haile Selassie I, or to outwardly identify with the descendants of ancient Hebrews whose men were usually depicted as fully bearded. By the 1940s, dreadlocks emerged as an essential element of Rastafarian identity, especially among young Rastas with an interest in breaking with traditional tenets of Jamaican society (see Figure 6).

Rastafarian oral traditions provide multiple answers regarding what inspired the first dreadlocks. Some attribute the source of inspiration to the appearance of African tribesmen (Gallas, Somalis, Massais) or Mau Mau fighters with similar hairstyles in Jamaican newspapers. One conjecture suggests that the pictures

6. Dreadlocked Fisherman

of Hindu holy men, known as Sadhus, provided the primary inspiration. Rastas often cite biblical injunctions against the cutting of hair and the shaving of beards among the Nazarites (Hebrews who undertook a special vow of consecration to God), as set forth in Numbers 6 and as exemplified by Samson in Judges 13 and 14, as the inspiration and justification for their hairstyles. Concerning the actual inception of the dreadlocks hairstyle in Jamaica, the oral traditions give two answers. The first credits Howell's fearsome guardsmen who patrolled the boundaries of his commune at Pinnacle. They reportedly cultivated this hairstyle to accentuate the 'dread' they wished to inspire in anyone who dared to breach Pinnacle's perimeter. The second ascribes the origin of dreadlocks to young Rastas of the 1940s who repudiated the Babylonian culture of Jamaica even more radically than their elders, who defied the usual clean-cut image by growing long beards and hair but still groomed themselves with scissors and combs. The latter tradition, supported by ethnographic research, has had currency in Rastafarian studies in recent years, but in the absence of documented sources from the 1930s and 1940s, determining the validity of competing claims from an oral culture is almost impossible.

The dreadlocks hairstyle is one of the most symbolically rich elements of Rastafari. It signals a determined embrace of African features as beautiful and a desire to accentuate them. While European standards of beauty celebrated finer hair texture, lighter skin tones, and careful grooming, Rastas renounced these norms by cultivating their so-called 'nappy' hair into the knotted locks that came to symbolize Rastafari. Closely related to the acceptance of African beauty is the commitment to naturalness that dreadlocks symbolize. According to Rastas, one of the most despicable traits of Babylon is its predilection for the artificial. This preference for the artificial shows up among black people who resort to hot combs and chemicals to attain straighter and finer textured hair, and thus the approximation of whiteness. In the estimation of Rastas, such a practice demonstrates an alienation from the natural African self and a desire for an unattainable whiteness. Such artificiality is, by definition, out of sync with the natural principles that Jah has ordained.

Considered a simulation of the lion's mane, dreadlocks symbolize confidence, boldness, and uprightness. Rastas' adoption of the lion as a symbol of their character is intended to expunge the stereotypically weak, fickle personality that oppressive systems in the Americas have foisted upon blacks. It rejects the obsequious and morally vacillating Anansi of Jamaican folklore, the diffident and compliant peasant called Quashie, and the passive and subservient American Uncle Tom. Imbibing and projecting lion-ness not only speaks to the inward fortitude and outward fearlessness of Rastas, but also the profound fear and apprehension that dreadlocks are likely to inspire in 'baldheads' (non-Rasta). 'Dread' locks are supposed to make the weak-hearted quake, or become fearful of the bold, assertive Rastas. Taking on the character of a lion also identifies Rastas with Haile Selassie I, who bore the title 'Conquering Lion of the Tribe of Judah', whose astral sign was Leo, whose royal seals had lions engraved on them, and whose palace entrances were guarded by statues of lions. Because Haile Selassie I was often pictured with lions, Rastas have conjured tales of pet lions roaming the grounds of the royal palace.

In addition to its identification of Rastas with Selassie, the dreadlocks hairstyle is a mark of InI consciousness and a connection of the individual to Jah's power that pervades the universe like radio waves. Similar to the Hindu belief that Brahman pervades the universe, Rastas insist that the power of Jah is immanent in the world. They call this power 'earthforce' and regard their locks as sensory devices that can tap into this force, transmit it, and channel its power, whether for creative or for destructive purposes. Hence, the 'flashing of the lock' is associated with the unleashing of destructive forces against the Babylon system.

Dreadtalk, as an in-group language that surfaced among Rastas in the 1940s, was born out of a need to have a vocabulary that could faithfully describe the experience of Rastafari and convey the evolving consciousness of its members. Finding the English language inadequate and drawing inspiration from their ganja-induced state of mind, Rastas engaged in the task of remaking the English language and the Jamaican patwa (patois) into a potent instrument for expressing their own perspective. For example, a plethora of 'I' words expresses their understanding of the presence of divine positive energy in the world: 'InI' for the divine unity of God and humans; 'ital' for natural or organic foods; 'irie' for positive feelings or vibrations; 'Iman' for the Rasta who is conscious of his inner divinity; 'inity' for unity; and 'irator' and 'iration' for the Creator and the creation. In this way, the Rastas have used language to fashion another tool in the enterprise of 'chanting down Babylon'.

The conviction that the English language was an instrument of Western oppression that robbed Africans of their native speech was central to the creation of an in-group language. Instead of aspiring for the social mobility associated with mastering the nuances of English and mouthing the cadences of diction

Velma Pollard on dreadtalk

Velma Pollard, the foremost scholar of Rastafarian speech, identifies the following features of the linguistic innovations of dreadtalk:

1. The creation of new 'I' words and expressions such as *Irie* for good or fine, *Iman* for I, me, or my, and *InI* for we or you and I.

2. The replacement of the initial syllable of words with 'I' as in *ital* for natural or vital, *irate* or *iration* for create or creation, and *ilaloo* for calaloo.

3. The investing of English or patwa words with specific Rastafarian meanings, so that 'forward' now means to leave, go, or come; 'seen' now means yes, I agree, or I perceive what you are saying; and 'reason' can mean to talk or discuss, or can be used as reference to the dialogue in which Rastas engage while they are participating in the communal smoking of ganja.

4. The replacement of some syllables considered contrary to the meaning of the words (usually based on their sounds) with syllables considered more appropriate; for example, oppress becomes *downpress*; dedicate becomes livicate; understand becomes overstand; UC (University College, the precursor of University of the West Indies) became *ublain* (you blind) to indicate that the university was not helping people to see the truth, but blinding them through Babylon education.

associated with the Oxford or Cambridge educated, Rastas have launched an ideological attack on the integrity of the English language. Drawing on an African tradition of viewing words as having intrinsic power, potent vibration, and effective agency, they articulated the philosophy of 'word, sound and power'. Generally, this indicates that the phonetics of words should be closely aligned with their meanings. From this perspective, Rastas found pervasive confusion and corruption of sounds and meanings in the English language. The word 'oppression', for example, signifies the utter restriction of freedom and equality. Yet the first syllable is pronounced with the positive sounding 'up'. From the perspective of Rastafarian linguistic sensibilities, what English calls oppression is really pressure on the poor by those in a higher social position, and therefore 'downpression' is the correct term to capture the significance of their activities. A word like 'dedicate' is also subject to change; though the definition is positive, it begins with the negative syllable 'ded' (dead) and is more accurately represented by the word 'livicate'.

Livity: natural living

While individual Rastas have the freedom to fashion their lifestyles based on their understanding of the Creator, themselves, and Rastafari, the concept of livity or natural living has wide currency within the movement. For many, the key building block for a truly Rastafarian lifestyle is a commitment to the use of natural rather than manufactured and especially artificial products. This is based on the Rastafarian conviction that health and longevity emanate from the organic properties with which Jah has imbued the natural environment. Altering the dynamics of nature with chemicals and manufacturing techniques leads to human ill-health and environmental degradation. Rastas declare that 'Ital is vital – the natural is life-giving'. The 'ital' principles of Rastafari put a premium on the use of natural and organic foods, and show preference for locally grown grains, fruits, and vegetables. For the strictest of Rastas, this translates into a rigorous vegetarianism free from processed foods: all canned goods, all refined flours and sugars, all additives, and even salt. Others are less rigid, eating some meat and fish under one foot long because long fishes are considered predatory (an essential trait of Babylon). However, most subscribe to the food laws of the ancient Hebrews found in Leviticus 11 and avoid pork, fish without scales, and all kinds of crustaceans.

An essential component of natural living is the utilization of the healing power of herbs. Jamaican Rastas in particular avail themselves of a variety of herbs gathered from the wild or cultivated in their gardens. These, they believe, provide the natural energy and healing properties to ensure perpetual physical health and mental clarity. For Rastas, ganja (cannabis sativa or marijuana) is the supreme herb. They ingest it as a tea, as an ingredient in medicinal concoctions, as a spice in cooking, and most importantly in ritual and recreational smoking. While Rastas forbid the use and abuse of manufactured drugs and substances such as cocaine, heroin, alcohol, and even cigarettes, ganja is regarded as a plant whose use was ordained by Jah for human wellbeing. Rastas frequently cite Genesis 1:29 as justification for the their use of ganja: 'And God said, Behold, I have given you every herb bearing seed, which is on the face of all the earth, and every tree, in the which is the fruit of a tree yielding seed; to you it shall be for meat'. Further justification is extrapolated from Revelations 22:2: 'On each side of the river stood the tree of life, bearing twelve crops of fruit, yielding its fruit every month. *And the leaves of the tree are for the healing of the nations*' (NIV). In this case, the interpretive genius of Rastafari identifies the 'tree of life' as the ganja plant (see Figure 7).

Rastas eulogize ganja smoking for its ability to induce a feeling of peace and love. This is in contrast to the contention of law enforcement authorities who vilify ganja as a dangerous drug that disposes its users to violence and criminality. For Rastas, the ritual smoking of ganja is a celebration of fellowship and communal

7. Smoking of ganja

bonds. Ritual smoking is considered the taking of the chalice, associating it with the taking of the bread and wine that celebrates communion among Christians. Beyond its role in creating and maintaining communal bonds, ganja smoking facilitates personal introspection that leads to the discovery and exploration of InI consciousness. It is the vehicle that leads one through the distorted cultural landscape of Babylon and the false consciousness spawned by its oppressive institutions to a discovery of the true self, the divine I capable of self-direction. Interestingly, ganja smoking is usually the precursor to growing dreadlocks and the declaration of Rastafarian identity.

Legalization of ganja?

In 2000, the Jamaican government appointed the National Commission on Ganja, which was chaired by Barry Chevannes, a well established scholar of Rastafari and then dean of the social sciences department at the University of the West Indies at Mona, Jamaica. Though stopping short of calling for the full legalization of ganja, the commission recommended its decriminalization. Here is a summary of the commission's recommendations:

1. that the relevant laws be amended so that ganja be decriminalized for the private, personal use of small quantities by adults;
2. that decriminalization for personal use should exclude smoking by juveniles or by anyone in premises accessible to the public;
3. that ganja should be decriminalized for use as a sacrament for religious purposes;
4. that a sustained all-media, all-schools education programme aimed at demand reduction should accompany the process of decriminalization, and that its target should be, in the main, young people;
5. that the security forces intensify their interdiction of large cultivation of ganja and trafficking of all illegal drugs, in particular crack/cocaine;
6. that, in order that Jamaica be not left behind, a Cannabis Research Agency be set up, in collaboration with other countries, to coordinate research into all aspects of cannabis, including its epidemiological and psychological effects, and, importantly, its pharmacological and economic potential, as is being done by many other countries, not least including some of those that are the most vigorous in its suppression; and
7. that, as a matter of great urgency, Jamaica should embark on diplomatic initiatives with its CARICOM partners and other

countries outside the region, in particular members of the European Union, with a view to (a) elicit support for its internal position; and (b) influence the international community to re-examine the status of cannabis.

The full report can be found online (at http://www.cannabis-med.org/science/Jamaica.htm). Though the Jamaican government initially indicated its support for the recommendations, opposition from churches in Jamaica and from the United States government pushed the issue from the nation's legislative agenda.

Certain elements of Rastology and livity, such as the deification of Haile Selassie I, dreadtalk, and the cultivation of dreadlocks, have been discounted by critics of Rastafari as inspired by the inebriation of those who have consumed ganja in excess. However, a closer look will reveal that Rastafari, though steeped in the symbolic and the mythic, represents a commitment to reconstitute an African self that has been trampled by slavery and Western cultural imperialism. Rastafari represents a people disaffected by and dissatisfied with the forces of Western civilization, which have assigned them a place in the margins of history and society. Drawing on the cultural resources of their African past and the myth-making capacity shared by humans, they have created a movement and a culture that represents their sense of self as divine and empowered. And, remarkably, the spread of its music, art, and literature has catapulted Rastafari into becoming a cultural force in Jamaica and the world. Maya Angelou's poem, *Still I Rise*, accurately captures the essence of what Rastafari represents: 'You may write me down in history / With your bitter, twisted lies / You may trod me in the very dirt / But still, like dust, I'll rise'.

Chapter 3

Grounding, houses, and mansions: social formation of Rastafari

Rastafari is not a homogenous movement with the ability to regulate the beliefs and behaviour of its members. It has no single administrative structure or leadership hierarchy to define and enforce orthodoxy. In this respect, Rastafari is less like Christian denominations, with clearly articulated doctrines and a centralized, entrenched leadership hierarchy, and more like other African diaspora religious traditions, whose formations are of a cellular nature. Folk religions such as Vodou in Haiti, Santeria in Cuba, and Revival Zion in Jamaica tend to consist of autonomous groups that function independently. Without been linked by hierarchical organizational structures, they relate to one another through personal relationships, if at all. The social formation of Rastafari exhibits a similar web-like or reticulate structure. It is a network of individuals and groups joined by personal relationships and a shared cultural ethos.

The heterogeneity of Rastafari social formation

The lack of centralized hierarchical structures in Rastafari arises primarily from two aspects of the movement. The first is Rastafari's rejection of the formal structures of Babylon's institutions (politics, economy, education, church, law enforcement) that Rastas deem oppressive and repressive of individual initiative and creativity. To replicate these structures within

Rastafari would be tantamount to adopting the structures against which they are rebelling. Second, the concept of InI imbues members of the movement with an ultra individualism that resists bureaucratic and hierarchical organization, and fosters an epistemology that privileges the intuitive self over authority figures or rational organizations. Since to be Rastafari means to become conscious of one's innate divine essence and hence to reestablish a mystical union with Jah, Rastas have no need of priests to mediate between them and God or preachers to propound the truth to them. The conscious 'I' aware of his/her mystical union with Jah is also the seeing 'eye' that apprehends through divine inspiration. Hence knowledge and truth comes by direct divine inspiration, not from a professionally trained clergy.

Steeped in this kind of doctrinal individualism, many Rastas refuse to identify with any group and pursue Rastafari solo. For them, their spirituality focuses on the consciousness of their divine, African selves and the lifestyle that emerges from that awareness. They may embrace all of the elements of the general Rastafarian worldview, or they may reject particular aspects of Rastalogy and develop their distinctive and personal understanding of their faith. They may fashion a lifestyle based on all those elements of 'livity' that have emerged in the movement over the years, or they may have their own idiosyncratic approach to living out the Rastafarian conviction. For example, between the late 1970s and January of 2011, I encountered several Rastas who believe, unlike a significant majority of Rastas, that Haile Selassie I was a mere mortal. He was, they explain, a great pan-Africanist and an advocate for black liberation, but not a divine personality. Other Rastas, Mutabaruka being the most prominent of these, claim that they do not partake in smoking ganja, despite its historical importance to Rastafari. They acknowledge that ganja is an aid to the discovery and exploration of InI consciousness. However, since they have already achieved such a high level of consciousness, smoking the holy weed is no longer necessary.

Obviously, such individualistic approaches to Rastafari engender heterogeneity which often leads to contestations concerning who is the most authentic Rasta.

Grounding as an expression of collectivity

Individualism notwithstanding, Rastas have developed forms of collective life centred around the notion of 'grounding'. Grounding indicates the establishment of relationships among like-minded Rastas. It is the shared sense of belonging and togetherness that comes from sustained contacts and intense interactions. Grounding is also the designation for the ritual activities and occasions through which circles or Rasta coalesce and perpetuate themselves. Activities such as ganja smoking, reasoning, dancing, and chanting to the rhythms of Rastafarian drumming are all grounding rituals; they are intended both to inculcate the attitude and outlook of

8. **Partaking of the chalice**

Rastafari in the minds of neophytes and to enable more established adherents to explore deeper 'overstanding' of themselves and the world. As expressed by a popular saying among Rastas, these ritual activities 'ground the nation [of Rastafari] to the essential foundation'. These activities are, therefore, the glue that cements a circle or group of Rastas together.

As discussed previously, Rastas regard ganja as a natural substance the use of which promotes social healing by producing a sense of peace and harmony among people; it assists in physical healing by energizing the body; and it facilitates psychological transformation by enabling the individual to break through false consciousness to discover the true divine self. Most Rastas smoke ganja and meditate daily to achieve these benefits. However, like minded Rastas gather frequently to partake of the holy herb together. The ritualized smoking and the significance of ganja have both African and Asian provenance. The African influence was mediated by 'Kumina', a spirit-possession ceremony prevalent in St. Thomas, where Leonard Howell spent much of his time during the incubation of Rastafari. Kumina was introduced by the Kongolese who were brought to Jamaica as indentured workers in the mid-1800s after the British abolished slavery. The smoking of ganja (which they called 'djamba' or 'diamba') during their religious ceremonies facilitates possession by the spirits of the ancestors. Indentured labourers brought from India between 1838 and 1917 also practiced the smoking of ganja in Hindu ceremonies. Regarded as a gift from the god Indra to heighten human consciousness (according to the *Rig Veda*), Indians in Jamaica smoked ganja in rites honouring Shiva and the goddess Kali. An Indian by the name of Laloo, who was spiritual adviser to the founding Rasta Leonard Howell, was probably responsible for introducing the ritual smoking of ganja and other elements of Hinduism into Rastafari. Even prior to the rise of Rastafari, the widespread use of ganja for medicinal and recreational purposes among Afro-Jamaicans may have resulted from its introduction by Indian indentured labourers and their descendants.

The most widely utilized method of ganja smoking in Jamaica, by Rastas and non-Rastas alike, is the oversized, conical ganja cigar or cigarette known as a spliff. But whenever two or more Rastas come together, their smoking tends to take on a ritual aura. One may roll a spliff and offer a prayer before lighting it. He proceeds to share the spliff with the others as they engage in a discussion of whatever topic occupies the forefront of their minds at that time. For more solemn occasions, Rastas utilize the 'chalice' (see Figure 8). The chalice may be one of three water pipes used in ritual smoking: 'kutchie' ('kochi'), said to be of African origin; 'chillum', originating in India; or 'steamer', constructed from bamboo and a small tin can. These pipes consist of a chamber for the prepared ganja, a water chamber, and a mouthpiece or stem. Utilizing the mouthpiece, the smoker draws the smoke through water (that functions as a kind of filter), inhales it into the lungs, and exhales it through the nostrils (and sometimes the mouth as well). Rastas have developed certain etiquettes and traditions surrounding the preparing and partaking of the chalice. This includes the preparation (cutting, blending, and moistening) of the substance on a 'suru' board (a piece of board reserved for this purpose), the removal of all head gears before the ceremony, the offering of prayers before the lighting of the pipe, and passing the pipe counter-clockwise around a circle of participating Rastas. For more traditional Rastas, who tend to hold tenaciously to a strict patriarchy, women are excluded from partaking of the chalice with men.

Accompanying the ritual smoking of ganja is the open-ended, dialogic, and probing conversation that Rastas call reasoning. Reasoning is an intense mental activity in which the participants seek to reach greater heights ('ites') of understanding ('overstanding') of whatever subject they are discussing. Topics may include any element of Rastafarian principles and practices or any items that the Rastas deem relevant. Current events, especially those involving the claims and activities of prominent political and religious leaders, are often the subject of analysis in Rastafarian reasoning. Though its purpose is not combative, reasoning may involve challenging the ideas or pointing out fallacies in the arguments that are put forth. As the participants explore deeper and deeper levels of meaning in their reasoning, each contributor pushes the boundary of understanding until the entire group achieves deeper or clearer insight into the topic under discussion. Rastas never elevate an insight to the status of an enduring creed, because at a later time or date, they will take up the topic once again and seek to push the boundary of apprehension and comprehension even further. Hence, the smoking of ganja and the reasoning that accompanies it give those gathered a chance to celebrate their oneness and explore their subjective yet shared understanding of themselves and the world.

Social and ritual grounding occurs most frequently 'where two or three are gathered' (Matthew 18:20) in the name of Jah to partake of the holy herb and to discuss the issues at hand, whether some matter internal to the group or the latest national or international event. For many, this occurs daily in particular locations, usually in the yards of respected elders. The position of elder does not necessarily carry any administrative functions or responsibilities. It is more of an honorific title informally bestowed upon those whose reputation for 'upful' (upright) livity and inspiring exposition of Rastalogy is unquestioned. An elder who has withstood harassment, beatings, and/or imprisonment at the hands of Babylon's agents for their uncompromising defence of Rastafari is held in even greater esteem by his immediate associates, as well as by the movement as a whole. While eldership is not a formal administrative position, elders are expected to provide guidance to others, foremost by an exemplary lifestyle. His house or yard is almost always the regular gathering place for the Rastas in his sphere of influence. He is expected to preserve discipline in his circle, and may devise a set of rules governing the behavior of those who wish to ground in his yard. Those who repeatedly contravene these rules are frequently banned from the circle. An elder is usually part of a network of other elders who plan movement-wide events and devise strategies to promote Rastafarian causes such as the legalization of ganja and repatriation.

In some cases, leading Rastas and their circles may convene regular or ad hoc gatherings that bring together scores of adherents. These are generally all-night events, where, in addition to ganja smoking and reasoning, Rastas engage in ritual drumming, chanting, and dancing. The music is played on a three-drum set known as the 'akete', but other percussion instruments such as rattles (maracas) and tambourines may provide accompaniment. The bass provides the foundation of the music and keeps the life line, while a mid-range drum called the 'fundeh' plays a syncopated rhythm. The 'peta' (repeater), a treble drum, improvizes over the rhythms laid down by the other two. The heavy beats of the bass in Rasta drumming (and in reggae) are symbolic blows against Babylon, while the lighter, more playful beats of the repeater denote hope. The tunes and lyrics of the songs chanted by the Rastas are generally based on traditional choruses and hymns sung in evangelical or Afro-Christian churches. Words are frequently modified or inserted to make the songs conform to Rastafarian perspectives, to express the experiences and aspirations of Rastas, and to convey their praise of Haile Selassie I or Jah Rastafari. A typical example of Rastafarian drumming and chanting is heard on 'Rastaman Chant', recorded and popularized by Bob Marley and the Wailers. It was originally a Christian chorus called 'I'll Fly Away to Glory', but was later modified by Rastas during their grounding ceremonies. Eventually, Bob Marley added it to his repertoire. Above the bubbling drum rhythms, Marley sings, 'Hear the words of the Rastaman say, Babylon, yuh [your] throne gone down, gone down; Babylon, yuh throne gone down'. At grounding ceremonies, dancers usually gather around the drummers and/ or a bonfire and mark time to the heavy bass rhythms. More excited Rastas may engage in a more energetic display of jumping and spinning, as Bob Marley was disposed to do during his performances.

The largest grounding of Rastas, called 'groundations' or 'grounations' in the 1950s, are now referred to as Nyabinghi

Assemblies (Issemblies). The term 'Nyabinghi' is of East African origin, referring to a legendary (and probably mythical) African queen who led resistance against invaders. In times of incursion by foreigners, the spirit of Nyabinghi was believed to possess female warriors who then led the effort to repel the invaders. In the early twentieth century, the spirit of Nyabinghi appeared in the person of Muhumuza, a woman who led a resistance movement against the European (German, Belgian, and British) penetration of the Congo, Uganda, and Rwanda. Knowledge of Nyabinghi probably reached Jamaica via a propaganda article by the Italian journalist, Frederico Philos, first published in Italy in 1934 and later republished in the *Jamaica Times* in 1935. The article, a sensationalist piece intended to bolster European efforts against African resistance to colonialism, averred that there was a pan-African secret organization called 'Nya-Binghi' whose declared purpose was 'Death to all Whites'. Furthermore, the article claimed that Emperor Haile Selassie I was appointed supreme leader of this group in a secret Moscow meeting in 1930. Black people, wrote Philos, had accorded Selassie a messianic status and offered him intemperate devotion.

When Philos's claims were reported in Jamaica, Rastas overlooked the racist propaganda and embraced the concept of Nyabinghi as 'death to white oppressors', later restated as 'death to black and white oppressors'. Nyabinghi soon became the designation of the general gathering of Rastas. The activities at this gathering, including the drumming style, also known as Nyabinghi drumming, are said to release mystical powers that work to destroy whites and their Babylon system. The branch of Rastafari committed to the most traditional principles of Rastafari, particularly a refusal to compromise with Babylon, is also called Nyabinghi or House of Nyabinghi.

The roots of Nyabinghi assemblies (Binghi for short) can be traced to Pinnacle, where Howell held periodic celebrations attended by many Rastas who were not domiciled in the commune. When the ferment of Rastafari shifted to West Kingston in 1940s and 1950s some general gatherings were probably held there. However, it seems that Rastas preferred the densely wooded Wareika Hills to the east of the city where they could retreat for assemblies, escaping the gaze and likely harassment of the law enforcement in the city. By the late 1950s, Nyabinghi assemblies had become an essential feature of the Rastafarian movement, evidenced by the highly publicized 'Rasta Conventions' called by Prince Emmanuel Edwards in 1958 and by Claudius Henry in 1959.

Over the years, Rastas have sanctified several dates on the calendar for Nyabinghis. Most of these are connected with Haile Selassie I and Ethiopia: Ethiopian Christmas on 7 January, the anniversary of Selassie's visit to Jamaica on 21 April, the founding of the Organization of African Unity (initiated by Selassie) on 26 May, Selassie's birthday on 23 July, the Ethiopian New Year on 11 September, and Selassie's coronation day on 2 November. Some also convene Nyabinghi assemblies for Emancipation Day (from the British) on 1 August and for Marcus Garvey's birthday on 17 August. Rastas from the Twelve Tribes of Israel tend to hold monthly celebrations and Rastas from the Bobo Shanti commune at Bull Bay to observe weekly Sabbaths. While Rastas from these groups may attend groundings on the above dates, these general assemblies are usually planned and executed by those who align themselves with the House of Nyabinghi.

The organizing and convening of a Nyabinghi Assembly illustrates the working of the informal but efficient network that characterizes Rastafari. First of all, anyone desiring to sponsor an assembly must be reputed for his faithful ('upful') pursuit of livity and an uncompromising defender of Rastafari. Moreover, he must command adequate resources to make a substantial contribution of resources (especially food) for the occasion. Indeed, if he or his family owns the property where the gathering will take place, he is considered more qualified as a sponsor. His desire to sponsor a Binghi is communicated to other Rasta elders who must offer their approval. Once this is settled among the elders, news of the impending Binghi is circulated throughout the movement by a vast network of personal relationships. On the appointed day, Rastas from all locales, including abroad, descend on the announced venue in huge numbers, laden with contributions to make the gathering a success.

Nyabinghi Assemblies typically last from three to seven days. They are generally convened in rural areas, either in the open air or under a temporary structure (temple or tabernacle) constructed for the occasion. During daylight hours, congregants prepare ital food or gather in circles to smoke ganja and engage in extended reasoning. At night, the drums dominate the proceedings as the faithful gather around bonfires to dance, sing praises ('ises") to Jah, and chant down Babylon until daylight. Inspired by copious consumption of ganja and pulsating rhythms that synchronize with the heartbeat, Rastas perform an ecstatic dance to deliver symbolic blows and release divine energy against Babylon by stomping on the ground and wildly flashing their dreadlocks.

As intimated earlier, Nyabinghi Assemblies have been associated with the struggle against the oppressive forces of Babylon. Rastas believe that their ritual actions during the assemblies are able to activate and deploy a mystical energy of Jah called 'earthforce' against forces of oppression. By the 1950s Nyabinghi Assemblies also became associated with repatriation. The assemblies convened by Prince Emmanuel Edwards in 1958 and Claudius Henry in 1959 were billed as a precursor to and preparation for repatriation. Today, both the downfall of Babylon and repatriation are invoked as the purposes of Nyabinghis. However, they are essentially occasions for establishing and maintaining solidarity among Rastas without recourse to formal creeds and hierarchical organizational structures. The gatherings not only create a sense of belonging within a greater collectivity, but also generate feelings of affinity and collective energy that confirm the congregants' conviction in the reality and veracity of Rastafari.

Houses and mansions

While the trenchant individualism of Rastas has militated against centralized organizational structures and codified doctrines, several distinct groups with particular orientations have emerged in the movement. Describing these groups is somewhat difficult because their structures exhibit much fluidity and the available ethnographic research on the various formations is severely limited. Nevertheless, the scholarship on Rastafari identifies the House of Nyabinghi, Twelve Tribes of Israel, and Bobo Shanti or Bobo Dreads as the major branches of Rastafari. The Church of Haile Selassie I, Inc., and, more recently, Fulfilled Rastafari are also important sects of the movement. Rastas recognize these groups as the 'houses and mansions' of Rastafari, alluding to the words of Jesus, 'In my father's house are many mansions' (John 14: 2, KJV).

The House of Nyabinghi is not a specific organization but an aggregation of Rastas who subscribe to the militant ethos of the movement that developed in the 1940s. That ethos anchors Rastafarian identity in the divinity of Haile Selassie I as the messiah in his second appearance. Rastas of the Nyabinghi persuasion valorize dreadlocks as indispensable to a true Rasta. They are more likely to pursue a strict ital or vegan diet ('livet') and to eschew entanglement with Babylon's economic and political system. For example, many in the Nyabinghi ethos view reggae as a bastardization of Rasta music and contend that Bob Marley's involvement with the capitalist recording industry of Babylon was a betrayal of Rastafarian livity. Ironically, this branch of Rastafari takes its name from Nyabinghi, the legendary African queen, and yet it subjects women to male authority and excludes them from the circle of males during the ritual smoking of ganja. The House of Nyabinghi is probably the largest subdivision of Rastafari and operates through the inspirational leadership of elders, whose main functions are to provide guidance to their circles, represent the interests of Rastafari to wider society, and organize Nyabinghi assemblies and other Rastafarian activities.

The house of Bobo Shanti or Bobo Dreads traces its roots to the formation of the Ethiopia Africa Black International Congress (EABIC) by Prince Emmanuel Edwards in the 1950s (see Figure 9). Though the exact date of this group's founding is uncertain, it came to prominence in 1958 when Prince Emmanuel I or King Emmanuel I, as Edwards is called by his followers, convened a large gathering of Rastas in Kingston. Some disagreement exists among scholars concerning the derivation of the term 'Bobo Shanti'. One suggestion is that it is the combination of the Hindi word 'baba', meaning 'father,' and 'shanthi', meaning 'love' or 'peace.' It is more likely, however, that the name originated from the West African word 'bobo', meaning black, and the Ashanti tribe, which was noted for its fierce warriors and from which

9. **King Emmanuel, founder of the Bobo Ashanti House of Rastafari**

numerous slaves were reportedly taken to Jamaica. Bobo Dreads are readily identifiable by their long flowing robes and characteristic head wrap (turban), often black, white, and other bold colours.

After his compound in Ackee Walk, West Kingston, was razed by government bulldozers in 1966, Edwards and his followers moved several times before settling in the hills above Bull Bay, where they established a commune on government owned land. Essentially, this group revolves around Edwards, whose charismatic personality has dominated the group since its founding and even after his death in 1994, at which point Trevor Stewart became the new high priest. Edwards promulgated a new trinity in which Haile Selassie is the living God-King, Edwards himself is Christ or the high priest, and Marcus Garvey is the prophet. The male followers are categorized into two groups: the priests who conduct the weekly religious rites and services, and the prophets who engage in reasoning to explore greater understanding of the principles of Rastafari. Male members are assigned other necessary functions such as guarding the gate, servicing the generator that provides power, keeping the store house, and purchasing supplies.

In their commune above Bull Bay, the Bobo Dreads developed an even more rigid ethos than the Nyabinghis. This involves a frugal lifestyle based on subsistence farming and making brooms to sell. They prostrate themselves in prayer several times a day, attend nightly services in the meeting yard, fast at least twice every week, and observe Sabbath services in their temple. Sabbath services are lengthy affairs that involve drumming, ritual smoking of ganja, singing, and Bible readings. The high priest generally gives a sermon in the style of a running commentary on Bible verses read aloud by one of the priests. Sermons tend to focus on proving the tenets of Rastafari, namely that God has arrived in the persons of Selassie I and Emmanuel Edwards, blacks are divinely chosen and thus superior to whites, whites are bent on oppression and exploitation, and the kingdom of Babylon is doomed to destruction. Shouts of 'Holy Emmanuel I, Selassie I, Jah Rastafari', or similar phrases, frequently punctuate the singing and sermons.

Bobo Dreads' patriarchal system brands women as distracting to men's spiritual pursuit and they are thus relegated to the background of communal life, where they are responsible only for raising children and domestic chores. Their clothing must cover their arms, legs, and heads at all times when they are in the presence of men. Because of their perceived impurities, they are also not allowed to cook for men. As menstruation and childbearing are the main sources of their impurity, women must stay in seclusion for the entire duration of their menstrual periods as well as several days before and after and for three months after giving birth.

While Bobo Dreads are associated with their Bull Bay commune, some have lived outside, and increasingly so since 1990s, especially after the passing of Prince Emmanuel Edwards. Bobo Shanti has also acquired an international following in places such as Trinidad and Tobago, the United States, and England. How the communal ethos developed at Bull Bay applies to Bobo Dreads residing outside the community and abroad is unclear. However, Bull Bay has become a pilgrimage site that these Rastas might visit as they desire, especially for significant celebrations. They are also known to make financial contributions for the upkeep of the commune. A growing number of 'conscious' reggae artists have aligned themselves with Bobo Shanti. Whereas the celebrated reggae artists of the 1970s tended to be members of the Twelve Tribes of Israel, since the mid-1990s this has changed with Bobo Dreads such as Capleton, Anthony B, Sizzla, Lutan Fiyah, Fantan Mojah, Jah Mason, Junior Kelly, and Ras Shiloh.

The Twelve Tribes of Israel mansion was founded in 1968 by Vernon Carrington, who claimed to be the reincarnation of Gad, one of the twelve sons of Israel (Jacob). Carrington, called Prophet Gad or Gadman by his followers, claimed that he was reading the

Bobo Shanti in transition

The death of the patriarch of the Bobo Dreads, Prince Emmanuel Edwards, in 1994 constituted two crises for the community: a challenge to the belief that righteous Rastas in general and Prince Emmanuel in particular could not die; and a void in leadership, with no prescribed procedure for choosing a successor. Initially, the community did not accept the finality of Prince Emmanuel's passing and reportedly left the body in place for three days waiting for it to be miraculously resuscitated as was Jesus Christ in the Bible. Eventually, reality took hold and the body was buried. The greater issue was then the question of who would succeed Prince Emmanuel as patriarch and spiritual head of the community. While Trevor Stewart initially assumed leadership two groups have left the original commune to establish their own settlements further up the mountains with the leader of each group claiming to be the inheritor of Prince Emmanuel's authority.

Bible when he received a special call from God/Jah to reunify the lost tribes of Israel. Thus, his followers are assigned to one of those twelve tribes. Membership is not assigned by traceable ancestry but by the month of one's birth, following the Hebrew religious calendar that begins in April and ends in March. Each tribe is associated with a certain colour, body part, and mental function or capacity. For example, Bob Marley belonged to the tribe of Joseph because he was born in February; his colour was white; his body part was the calf; and, fittingly, his mental capacity was imagination.

The Twelve Tribes of Israel has not elaborated many distinctive teachings or practices. The basic responsibility that is incumbent on the Twelve Tribes Rasta is to 'read a chapter [of the Bible] a day'. Fashioning a Rastafarian lifestyle is mostly left upto the individual. While cultivating dreadlocks and pursuing ital livity

Twelve Tribes of Israel

The Prophet Gad (aka Vernon Carrington), founder of the Rastafarian group called the Twelve Tribes of Israel, believed that his mission was to reconstitute the ancient Hebrew tribes that bore the names of the sons of Jacob. Based on their birth month all the members are assigned to a tribe and associated with a certain characteristic:

Tribe	Birth Month	Characteristic
Reuben	April/*Nisan*	Strength
Simeon	May/*Iyar*	Faith
Levi	June/*Sivan*	Will
Judah	July/*Tammuz*	Praise
Issachar	August/*Av*	Zeal
Zebulon	September/*Elus*	Order and compassion
Dan	October/*Tishri*	Judgement
Gad	November/*Heshvan*	Power
Asher	December/*Kislev*	Understanding
Napthali	January/*Tevet*	Love
Joseph	February/*Shevat*	Imagination
Benjamin	March/*Adar*	Elimination

are commendable, they are not viewed as requirements. While the Prophet Gad never cut or shaved his hair, he groomed it using a comb, a practice rejected by Nyabinghi Rastas

The Twelve Tribes are often dubbed 'Christian Rastas', because while other Rastas tend to repudiate Jesus, associating him with the *Jesus of Lubeck*, one of John Hawkins' slave ships, Twelve Tribes members insist that Jesus Christ (Yahshuah) of the New Testament is the messiah and the only saviour of humankind. To them, Selassie was a divine king in the line of David, fulfilling the biblical prophecy, 'The scepter shall not depart from Judah, nor a lawgiver from between his feet until Shiloh come, and unto Him shall the gathering of the people be' (Genesis 49:10, KJV). He was a twentieth century representative of Jesus Christ, but he was not the expected messiah who will return in the bodily form in which he ascended into heaven. At that time, he will come to pass judgement and to rule the earth.

Since its peak in the 1970s, Twelve Tribes has been reputed for attracting middle class followers with college or university educations and especially musicians and artists. For this reason, they are often referred to as 'middle class Rastas', and 'uptown Rastas' after Prophet Gad moved his headquarters to the more affluent Hope Road location, not far from Bob Marley's residence. Somewhat less Afrocentric than their counterparts in the Nyabinghi and Bobo Shanti orders, Twelve Tribes maintains that salvation is open to all and therefore accepts members from other races. White Rastas are therefore more likely to belong to this mansion than to any others, though some have embraced Nyabinghi. This accessibility has contributed to the spread of Twelve Tribes throughout the Caribbean, North America, several European countries, many regions of Africa, and New Zealand.

While the Twelve Tribes mansion has some semblance of organization – the appointment of shepherds to oversee various tribes or groups and the establishment of a twelve-member executive council – it was Gad's directives that governed the Twelve Tribes. However, he was not given to issuing copious directives. Apart from the requirement to read a chapter of the Bible every day, Twelve Tribes members have been basically free to pursue their individual understanding of Rastafari. Since Gad's passing in 2005, authority has passed to the executive council, which has so far avoided making waves in the movement.

While the House of Nyabinghi, the Bobo Shanti, and the Twelve Tribes of Israel are recognized as the major 'mansions' of Rastafari, numerous other 'houses' exist. One of the most well known is the Church of Haile Selassie I (Ba Beta Kristiyan Haile Selassie I) with branches in Jamaica, the United States, England, Haiti, Barbados, and Trinidad. Organized by Abuna (aka

Ascento) Foxe in conjunction with the Imperial Ethiopian World Federation, the Church of Haile Selassie I operates very much like a Christian church. They have a hierarchy of functionaries, weekly services, and Sunday schools. Foxe's aim is to foster the veneration of Haile Selassie in a manner similar to the worship of Christ in Christian churches, lending Rastafari the kind of respectability that might gain the recognition of the societies in which Rastas live and worship. In New York, for example, Foxe and others have been able to function as chaplains in the prison system.

Though its genesis and history are unclear, a new house of Rastafari called Fulfilled Rastafari has been making its presence known in recent years, especially via the Internet. Based on their web posts, they have a multi-ethnic membership in the United States and England. Similar to Twelve Tribes, Fulfilled Rastas leave the issues of dreadlocks and ital livity up to the individual, though they have declared their belief that God wants us to live in harmony with nature. Their central emphasis is following Christ as taught by Haile Selassie I. They therefore take to heart Selassie's own insistence that he was merely a man and a Christian. Selassie's speeches and writings seem to be their main source of inspiration. Accordingly, they have a strong commitment to peace, justice, and tolerance in the human family

Among Rastas, the desire to create a central organization has circulated since the 1970s. Some contend that this unity would promote Rastafarian interest, protect the Rastafarian image, and facilitate the development of Rastafarian communities. This desire inspired the formation of the Rastafari Movement Association in the 1970s, envisioning the mobilization of Rastas as a political force in Jamaica. The various international assemblies of Rastafari, beginning with the first meeting in Toronto in 1982, were all part of the attempt to create a unified, global Rastafari movement. However, thus far, nobody seems able to establish a cohesive organization and purpose in Rastafari. Even if some Rastas, likely the most educated, are able to come together to form a movement-wide organization, the greater task would still remain the grassroots work of integrating local Rastas under its umbrella. So far, no one has emerged with the skill, drive, and determination necessary to accomplish such a feat.

Chapter 4
Rastafari international: the making of a global movement

In 'I Shot the Sheriff', Bob Marley sings of a Sheriff John Brown who gives orders for every seed Marley plants to be destroyed before it has a chance to germinate. The most obvious allusion is to the efforts of Jamaican authorities to stamp out the growing and use of ganja, which is an essential part of Rastafarian ritual. However, given his penchant for multi-vocality, Marley is probably also alluding to repressive measures by law enforcement against Rastafari. Despite these measures in Jamaica and elsewhere, Rastafari has grown from its obscure beginnings in Jamaica in the early 1930s to become an international movement in the twenty-first century. Estimates put the number of Rastas at between 700,000 and 1,000,00 worldwide. While these numbers cannot be verified, by the early years of the twenty-first century, adherents of Rastafari can be found in most of the major population centres and many outposts of the world. But the global significance of Rastafari goes far beyond the number of people who adhere to its principles and pursue its lifestyle. Its significance extends to the racial, political, and cultural consciousness it has fostered among African peoples in African diaspora as well as the African homeland, the inspiration it has provided for other dominated peoples (e.g, the Maori, the Hopi, and the Punjabi) to resist political and cultural domination, and its influence on musical and artistic production in the Caribbean and around the world. Rastafari can truly be considered an emerging world religion, if not in term of numbers, certainly in terms of global reach and influence. Though the research on the global spread and presence of Rastafari is still in its infancy, the growing ethnographic and journalistic data indicate that an interplay of migration, media, and 'missions' has facilitated its taking root in communities around the world.

Migration

The rebuilding efforts in Europe after World War II created job opportunities that attracted immigrants from the British West Indies to England in the 1950s and 1960s. Liberalized immigration laws in the United States and Canada fueled the emigration of many Caribbean residents to North America in the 1960s and 1970s. Along with other migrating Jamaicans, Rastas were disembarking in England by the mid-1950s. By the late 1950s, a group of Jamaican immigrants who had embraced Rastafari coalesced around such leading brethren as Ascento Foxe, Roy Prince, Bother Tull, and Brother Shaggy Berry and started establishing themselves in the Notting Hill area of West London. These immigrants were to exert considerable influence on the development of Rastafari in England.

By the late 1960s, the Rastafari movement in England was gaining a substantial following among the children of those who had immigrated to England in the 1950s and early 1960s. The social-psychological context of this embrace of Rastafari was disenchantment with Britain brought on by the economic hardships, racial discrimination in employment and housing, and social isolation that these second generation immigrants and their parents were experiencing. The intellectual context was the proliferation of black power ideas criticizing white oppression and calling for blacks to take control of their own communities and their political and economic future. While most Rastas seemed content to exist in the reticulate network that characterized Rastafari in Jamaica, others were committed to creating or participating in organizations geared towards the social improvement, cultural education, and political struggles of blacks in Britain. By the early 1960s, one element of the Rastafari movement in England had formed the Jamaican Working Committee to develop a more programmatic approach to addressing issues such as repatriation and defending the civil and human rights of blacks. Some of these same Rastas participated in the founding of the Universal Black Improvement Organization (UBIO) in 1969. Initially, UBIO was a diverse group of black activists holding an array of ideological and philosophical positions. But by the end of 1970, the leadership that was mostly Rasta ousted the intellectuals with other views (including Marxist) and imposed the perspective of Rastafari on the organization. Through the youth club of the UBIO, the Rastafarian leadership disseminated the principles of Rastafari and its version of African culture among children of black immigrants.

In 1971, UBIO morphed into the People's Democratic Movement (PDM) with the expressed purpose of mobilizing young people to take political and social action to facilitate their own development. Through such leaders as Amanuel (aka Ascento) Foxe and Norman Adams (Jah Blue), the PDM lobbied the New York and Jamaican leadership of the Ethiopian World Federation (EWF) to establish a branch of the EWF as well as the Ethiopian Orthodox Church in London. Local 33 was established in London in 1972 and the St Mary of Zion Ethiopian Orthodox Church was established in London in 1974. These organizations not only advocated for the interest of Rastas and other black immigrants, but also conferred a degree of legitimacy on Rastas. However, given the tendency towards fissiparity among Rastas, most Rastas refused to work within the confines of these organizations. Some found the political orientation of these groups antithetical to Rastafari; others objected to the insistence by some leaders (Foxe, for example) that Rastas should focus on gaining acceptance in Britain and on developing Jamaica instead of repatriation to Africa. Adding

73

to the sectarianism of Rastafari in Britain was the founding of a branch of the Twelve Tribes of Israel in London in 1972 by Judah Pepe; other branches were later established in other towns with sizable West Indian immigrant populations. Furthermore, groups of Rastas came together throughout England with the London organizations having very little or no direct influence or control over these groups.

The internationalization of reggae in the 1970s, with its acerbic criticism of white Western domination, its eulogizing of African heritage and African physical characteristics, and its call for resistance and rebellion against European cultural and aesthetic values, gave a significant boost to Rastafari in England. During his sojourn in London from 1976 to 1978 after an attempt on his life at his Hope Road residence in Jamaica, Bob Marley found fellowship in the growing Rastafarian community, especially among those who grounded with Norman Adams. Given his charisma and growing influence, Marley must have contributed to the strengthening of Rastafari in England. Rastafari mediated by reggae had a special resonance among the children of West Indian immigrants in search of their own identity in a society in which they felt alienated from the dominant British culture and in which they were often subjected to racist discrimination. Thus by the 1970s, Rastafari was well established in England, and despite social stigmatization and repressive measures by law enforcement authorities, it finally gained recognition as a legitimate culture group in the 1980s.

Social stress born of economic hardship and white conservative backlash against immigrants soon placed Rastas in the crossfire of media scrutiny and police harassment. By the mid to late 1970s, various newspapers had published reports characterizing Rastafari as a subculture of organized criminals comparable to the mafia. The infamous police report called *Shades of Grey*, published in 1977, gave credence to this characterization. Supposedly based on thorough investigation, the report asserted that an outbreak of criminal activities in the black enclave of Handsworth, Birmingham, was primarily the work of a group of 200 youths of West Indian descent with dreadlocks. This etched in the public's mind a correlation between dreadlocks/Rastafari and criminality or endemic sociopathy. The constant harassment of black youths by law enforcement officers sent to police their communities eventually erupted into the Brixton race riots of 1981 in which hundreds (including policemen) were injured and numerous buildings vandalized, looted, and burnt. A commission, chaired by Lord Scarman, that investigated the Brixton riots reported that Rastafarian teachings and actions were in no way responsible for the outbreak of violence, but suggested that Rastafari as a movement was susceptible to misuse by the criminally deviant. Shortly after the Scarman report, the Catholic Commission on Racial Justice issued a report in which it advocated the recognition of Rastafari as an authentic religious expression of a minority group. The Catholic Commission also urged the police to cease its aggressive and discriminatory policing of Rastafari and called on churches to enter into meaningful exchanges with Rastas. For their part, Rastas created organizations aimed at improving relationships with the British public and providing educational, cultural, and recreational services to black inner city youths. At the forefront of such Rastafarian initiatives were Rastafari Universal Zion piloted by Jah Bones, the Rastafarian Advisory Board founded by members of the Ethiopian World Federation, and the Rastafarian Women's Organization.

After the early 1980s, Rastas seemed to have settled into a somewhat routine existence in British society despite lingering tensions between Rastas and law enforcement and continuing negative perceptions of Rastafari by the public. In 1986, in an effort to counter continuing prejudices, the maturing Rastafarian community assisted by Carole Yawney, Canadian anthropologist and ardent advocate for Rastafari, organized 'Rastafari Focus', an international assembly of Rastas, to strengthen the local Rastafarian communities, to disseminate the truths about Rastafari to the public, and to enhance the international network of Rastafari. 'Rastafari Focus' was organized in conjunction with a year-long public celebration of Caribbean culture in Britain, and leading Rastas from Jamaica (Ras Boanerges and Miguel Lorne) and the eastern Caribbean travelled to London to participate in the proceedings. The successful challenge to discrimination against Rastas in the celebrated case of Trevor Dawkins in 1989 is also indicative of the maturing Rastafarian presence in Britain. Denied employment as a bus driver for a government transportation agency because he refused to cut his dreadlocks, Dawkins filed a discrimination grievance with the British Commission on Racial Equality. The commission ruled that the denial of employment to Dawkins was a violation of the 1976 Race Relations Act, and thus he was eligible for compensation. This ruling effectively conferred protection of Rastafari as an ethnic/religious group and stemmed the tide of systemic discrimination.

The same wave of migration that had established West Indian communities in England in the 1950s brought many Jamaicans to Canada and the United States in the 1960s. As in England, the Rastas were represented among these immigrants. Because Rastafari is so rooted in an oral culture, documentation of their presence and activities in the early days ranges from meagre to non-existent. Furthermore, no one has yet conducted the extensive ethnography that is necessary to uncover reliable information about the history of the movement in North America. Public documentation of the movement dates to the 1970s. Unfortunately, such documentation was disseminated by law enforcement and media outlets that peddled negativity and sensationalism. Police reports in New York in the 1970s and 1980s painted a portrait of Rastas as gratuitously violent (stimulated by marijuana smoking), deeply entrenched in organized crime, especially illegal drugs and gun trafficking, and politically dangerous because of their association with Marxist or Cuban organizations. Similarly, the association of Rastafari with violence and crime in Toronto led Canadian law enforcement to provocative policing of Rastas and West Indian immigrants in general, especially those involved in activist black organizations.

In 1983, the syndicated, investigative, and Pulitzer Prize-winning columnist Jack Anderson published a series of articles in the *Washington Post* and the *Philadelphia Daily News* on Rastafari. His assertion that Rastafari contained heavily armed Marxists poised to carry out attacks in the United States created jitters if not outright fear in the American public, especially in light of the geopolitics being waged between the United States and the Soviet Union in the Caribbean and Central America. Interestingly, none of his assertions were independently verified and none of his predictions ever materialized. However, these articles buttressed the ingrained fear of Rastafari both in North America and in the Caribbean, particularly the eastern Caribbean where activist Rastas were challenging the existing political structures. Though a *60 Minutes* feature on Rastafari in the 1980s utilized interviews of such Jamaican intellectuals as Rex Nettleford and Arthur Kitchen (himself a Rasta) to present a balanced perspective on the movement, this was soon followed by another *60 Minutes* report on the Ethiopian Zion Coptic Church, a fringe Rastafari group dominated by white Rastas residing in Florida. In the 1970s, this group was rumoured to control substantial resources supposedly gained through the growing and trafficking of ganja. Some of the white leaders of this group were convicted and imprisoned on ganja charges, leading to the breakup of the group in Florida and a decline of the group overall. The association of the Rasta-oriented group with the use and trafficking of an illegal substance furthered the negative image of Rastafari.

Despite the public negativity attached to Rastafari in North America, Rastas were able to pursue their way of life and add their cultural and political sensibilities to the tapestry of West Indian culture in North America, especially in large eastern cities such as Toronto, New York, Philadelphia, Washington, and Miami. Politically oriented Rastas joined immigrant and community organizations to resist the stigmatization of black immigrants and to advocate for fair treatment. Culturally oriented Rastas organized musical and artistic events featuring West Indian and Rastafarian culture. Reggae concerts were frequently held and clubs were established in communities with sizable West Indian populations. Stores and stalls selling Rasta-inspired wares (t-shirts, jewellry, arts and crafts) popped up in many neighbourhoods. Those most committed to the pursuit of Rastafarian spirituality formed circles of the like-minded in which they provide edification and inspiration for one another. Eventually, Rastas in North America replicated the various formations of Rastafari that emerged in Jamaica. Hence today in the United States and Canada we find circles of Rastas identifying themselves as Nyabinghi, Twelve Tribes of Israel, and Ethiopia Africa Black International Congress (aka Bobo Shanti), the main 'mansions' (branches or sects) of Rastafari in Jamaica. Some groups of Rastafari in North America tend to be more formally organized and to have more regular congregational gatherings. In this respect, the Church of Haile Selassie I seems to have gone the farthest towards regular, routine congregational activities. Organized in 1987 by Amanuel Foxe (aka Abuna Foxe) in the Bedford-Stuyvesant area of Brooklyn, New York, the Church of Haile Selassie I holds regular weekly services including congregational meetings and Sunday School. Foxe has also organized congregations of the Church of Haile Selassie I in London, Jamaica, Trinidad, Belize, and elsewhere, as well as establishing a presence on the Internet.

Another type of migration that has contributed to the spread of Rastafari is repatriation by individual Rastas to Africa. Repatriation to Africa in general and Ethiopia in particular is a fundamental tenet of Rastafari. Though no mass repatriation programme has been undertaken, individual Rastas, mostly from Jamaica and England, have 'resettled' in their ancestral homeland. Some have journeyed to West Africa to settle on a permanent or semi-permanent basis in a number of African countries. Ghana and Nigeria are favoured destinations.

For example, Rita Marley, wife of Bob Marley, now divides her time between Jamaica and Ghana. While Rastas have repatriated to various countries in Africa, the community of Rastas in Shashamane, Ethiopia, is the most celebrated case of repatriation. Since the 1960s, Rastas have been migrating to and settling on a 500 acre plot of land in the Shashamane Valley. As a gesture of thanks for the support he received from the African diaspora during his resistance to the Italian invasion and occupation of Ethiopia from 1935 to 1941, Haile Selassie made this land available through the Ethiopian World Federation to blacks in the West who wish to settle in Ethiopia. In general, Rastas regarded this land grant as part of the emperor's programme for their repatriation. While a few non-rastas such as James and Helen Piper took up settlement in Shashamane, the majority of settlers have been Rastas. Among the notable Rastafarian settlers arriving in Shashamane in the 1960s were Gladstone Robinson (1964), who was later appointed administrator of the settlement by the Ethiopian World Federation; Noel Dyer, who hitchhiked from England across Europe and North Africa for a year, arriving in Ethiopia in 1965; and Clifton and Inez Baugh, who made their journey in 1968. Despite conflicts with the local population, the confiscation of most of the 500 acres by the Marxist government of Mengistsu Haile Mariam after the deposing of Haile Selassie in 1974, and continued governmental opposition to their use of marijuana, Rastas have managed to maintain a presence at Shashamane. They have engaged in farming, created businesses, and established a school for their children and other children in the area. Ironically, the children of Shashamane Rastas now face a crisis of identity. Though born and raised in Ethiopia, they are essentially Western, and particularly Jamaican, since they have imbibed the cultural outlook of their parents. In fact, their status as Ethiopian citizens is even in question since they are considered foreigners in Ethiopia. At one point, the population of settlers in Shashamane was estimated at 2,000 with over 200 Rastafarian families. Over the years the numbers have gradually declined to an estimated 200 individuals.

Media

Modern media have been a most effective means of spreading
Rastafari around the world. In this regard, movies, reggae music,
and videos all contributed to the dissemination of the message of
Rastafari. The 1972 movie *The Harder They Come*, introduced
audiences in North America, Europe, Africa, and Asia to reggae and
the message of Rastafari. The movie exposed the underworld of
Jamaica's evolving music industry through the thwarted career of
the ambitious but frustrated Ivanhoe Martin (reggae artist Jimmy
Cliff). After being subjected to a series of exploitations, notably by
a music producer and those who controlled the local and
international ganja trade, Martin eventually shot a policeman who
was pursuing him and became a criminal folk hero and celebrated
recording artist who taunted the law enforcement officers while
being a fugitive. Though Rastafari appeared only tangentially in the
movie in the character Pedro (Ras Daniel Heartman), a ganja
dealer, the Rastafarian critique of Jamaican society permeates the
movie. On the sound track, such songs as 'The Harder They Come',
'You Can Get It If You Really Want', 'Rivers of Babylon', 'Johnny You
Too Bad', 'Many Rivers to Cross', and '007 – Shanty Town', all
reflected the prevailing incorporation of Rastafarian sentiments in
social commentary through the popular songs. As far afield as
Japan, people reported first becoming aware of reggae and
Rastafari through viewing *The Harder They Come*.

Following on the heels of *The Harder They Come*, reggae exploded
on the international scene. Fittingly, the album that ignited this
explosion was the Wailers' *Catch a Fire* (1973), with a cover
designed in the shape of a cigarette lighter. Interesting, Ras Daniel
Heartman had designed an earlier cover portraying all the Wailers
with Bob Marley in the centre smoking an over-sized spliff.
Obviously, Island Records considered Heartman's cover too radical
and opted for the more benign (but suggestive) cigarette lighter.
While Jamaican music had previously made ripples outside of
Jamaica—'My Boy Lollipop' by Millie Small in the UK in 1964,

'Israelites' by Desmond Dekker in the UK and US in 1968, and of course several of Jimmy Cliff's tracks on *The Harder They Come – Catch A Fire*, recorded by the Wailers and produced and promoted by Chris Blackwell of Island Records, made an enormous splash, marking the arrival of reggae on the world's stage. While many Jamaican solo artists and groups shared in the promotion of reggae and its Rastafarian-inflected message to the world, Bob Marley holds the distinction as the leading exponent of reggae and messenger of Rastafarian consciousness. As part of the Wailers trio with Bunny Livingston Wailer and Peter (McIn) Tosh (until Wailer and Tosh left the group), and later as Bob Marley and the Wailers, he released over ten albums on the Island Records label and toured extensively throughout North America and Europe. He also toured Japan, Australia, and New Zealand in 1979 and played several concerts in Africa in 1980, including his memorable performance at Zimbabwe's independence celebration, before his untimely passing in 1981 at the age of 36. On his albums and in his concerts, Marley focused his lyrical genius on addressing numerous subjects, but his lyrics are dominated by his reflection on his Rastafarian spirituality that celebrates Haile Selassie as the divine black liberator and by his trenchant critique of the social institutions of Western society as oppressive and alienating. He often urges his listeners to 'get up, stand up, stand up for your rights' ('Get Up, Stand Up') and to 'rebel, rebel, rebel now' ('Babylon System').

By the early 1970s, other Caribbean islands doubtless had some knowledge of Rastafari through media reports and through back and forth travel in the area, especially by students from other islands studying in Jamaica or Jamaicans studying in the eastern Caribbean. However, reggae music, with its Rasta-inspired, black consciousness lyrics inveighing against oppressive systems, was primarily responsible for the propagation of Rastafari in the eastern Caribbean. The message of reggae and Rastafari synchronized well with the anti-colonial and pro-Africa sentiments that prevailed in Trinidad, Grenada, Dominica, St. Vincent, and elsewhere during the 1970s. In this social milieu, militant groups of young Rastas, or Dreads as they call themselves in Dominica and St. Vincent, emerged with a penchant for political and cultural activism that outstripped their Jamaican counterparts. Rastas in Grenada participated in the 1979 revolution of the New Jewel Movement and occupied positions in the short-lived revolutionary government until it was plunged into internal fighting and overthrown by US military intervention in 1983. In the 1970s, the Dominican Dreads combined elements of Rastafari and Black Power ideology with progressive politics in challenging the legitimacy of the existing government and the entire political system. Viewed as dangerous, Rastafari was essentially outlawed by the governments of Dominica and St. Vincent. For example, after two Dreads were framed for the killing of a tourist in 1974, the Dominican government passed the Prohibition of Unlawful Societies and Association Act, aimed at stamping out Rastafari. In the ensuing years, the relationship between the Dreads and Dominican society was marked by a series of confrontations. Since the Acts effectively authorized the killing of Dreads by police and members of the public, the Dreads armed themselves and took to the hills from where they resisted police attempts to subdue them. The tensions eventually thawed somewhat after the repeal of the 'Dread Act' in the early 1980s. However, Rastas continued to be viewed as dangerous. Rastas from elsewhere were routinely denied entry into the Dominican Republic and children with dreadlocks were not accepted into government schools. Like the Dreads, the Trinidadian Rastas developed a reputation as social activists (without the violence) and became effective disseminators of the Rastafarian perspective through their publication, *Rasta Speaks*, which was first published in 1980 and became an international voice of Rastafari. Though its paper publication has ceased, *Rasta Speaks* continues to be a source of information and a forum for the discussion of Rastafarian perspectives online (rastaspeaks.com).

Cubans returning from working abroad as sailors, doctors, and agricultural advisers, and foreigners who went to Cuba to support the Revolution (*brigadistas*), first introduced reggae into Cuba. Jamaican and other Anglo-Caribbean students (including some Rastas), who received scholarships to study in Cuba in the 1970s, brought their reggae music collections with them and shared them with their Cuban counterparts. Other Cubans may have become acquainted with reggae by listening to it on radio broadcasts from Miami and Jamaica. Even though most Cubans could not understand the English or patwa (patois) lyrics of the songs, some, who later became Rastas, reported experiencing a sense of affinity to the rhythm and some claimed to have experienced a mystical flow of energy the first time they heard the music. The sense of confidence and rebellion that they discerned in the images of Rastas on album covers was also appealing.

By the 1980s, young Cubans started to hold what amounted to underground reggae parties in Havana and Santiago. Though their knowledge of Rastafari was elementary, some embraced the dreadlocks hairstyle. Eventually, Rastas from the eastern Caribbean and Guyana, who were studying in and near Havana in the 1990s, linked up with the dreadlocked youths in Havana and passed on some of the fundamental precepts of Rastafari. For Cuban Rastas, Rastafari gives them a way of asserting their blackness in a society that emphasized Cubanness as the identity of its people and discouraged any assertion of an African identity. Furthermore, though Cuba is socialist, its widespread economic hardship and its authoritarianism, especially through the policing of young, poor, and urban Afro-Cubans, amounts to a kind of Babylon in the eyes of those who embrace Rastafari.

Rastafari on the European continent, in such countries as France, Germany, Portugal, and the Netherlands, has established a foothold mostly among young black immigrants from Africa and the Caribbean, but has also attracted a growing number of whites. While personal contacts with Rastas from Britain and the Caribbean played a role in sowing the seeds in these countries, reggae, and particularly the music of Bob Marley, introduced the message of Rastafari to most of those who have adopted elements of the movement. The embrace of Rastafari falls on a continuum from serious engagement of Rastafari spirituality, to the deployment of Rastafari as a tool of resistance, to the adoption of Rastafarian symbols as a marker of African identity, to the 'consumption' of Rastafari as cool sub- or counter-cultural style. For adherents of African descent, the embrace of Rastafari tends to serve as a palliative for their sense of alienation fed by the racism and discrimination they encounter in their adopted homes. Whites tend to experience Rastafari as an alternative to and rejection of the stifling consumer and technology driven culture of their own societies.

Many adherents of Rastafari in west and southern Africa, Japan, New Zealand, Australia, Brazil, and elsewhere have reported that they were introduced to Rastafari by reggae music. In Japan, New Zealand, and Australia, Rastas point to the 1979 concerts by Bob Marley and the Wailers as turning points in their relationship to Rastafari. Even before seeing a Rasta in the flesh, youths in Russia, Mexico, Brazil, Israel, and among the Havasupai Indians in the Grand Canyon came to embrace aspects of Rastafari that they had gleaned from listening to reggae music.

In addition to reggae music, movies, videos, and the printed page have all facilitated the spread of information about and the message of Rastafari. Today, Rastas use the Internet to circulate information and to connect with like-minded people around the world. In addition to *Rasta Speaks*, sites such as *Africa Speaks* (africaspeaks.com) and *Rastafari Times* (rastatimes.com) make information about Rastafari available to the world. A Google search of the term 'Rastafari' will turn up more than 7.5 million pages with everything from historical information to forums for discussion of Rastafarian issues and concerns, to sites hawking Rasta-inspired wares, to news about reggae concerts and other cultural activities, to profiles of various Rastafarian houses and mansions and communities in numerous countries.

Missions

Though Rastafari is not a missionary religion in the conventional sense of recruiting and commissioning persons to proselytize others, Rastafarian elders from Jamaica have developed a tradition of 'trodding' (going on missions) to emerging Rastafarian communities to ground (instruct) new adherents in the fundamentals of Rastafari. 'Trodding' elders such as Ras Sam Brown, Mortimer Planno, and Ras Boanerges (aka Bongo Watto) have extended the reticulate network that characterizes the movement in Jamaica to the eastern Caribbean, North America, Europe, and Africa. As recognized stalwarts of Rastafari, they and others have received invitations or have taken the initiative to visit their often uninformed brethren and 'sistren' around the world to teach them the philosophy and practice of Rastafari. For example, Ras Boanerges, Ras Prophet, and Ikael Tafari (see Figure 9) travelled to Barbados in 1975 to acquaint Rastas there with the 'orthodox' Nyabinghi traditions that evolved in Jamaica. Ras Boanerges led a contingent of Nyabinghi elders to a number of the eastern Caribbean islands in 1983 to 'ground' with the brothers and sisters there. In 1984, Nyabinghi elders and some Rastafarian women were invited to Toronto to participate in the 'Voice of Thunder Dialogue'. For about a month, they not only sought to strengthen local Rastas, but also to educate the wider society about Rastafari in order to foster a more amiable relationship between Rastas and the public. In conjunction with 'Rastafari Focus' in London in 1986, Jamaican and other Rastas participated in the 'Nyabinghi Project' by conducting workshops in several British towns. Beginning with 'Rainbow Circle Throne Trod' of 1988, and followed by trods in 1989 and 1990, Jake Homiak, the Smithsonian anthropologist, ethnographer, and vigilant advocate for Rastafari, facilitated three 'missions' to the United States that included leading Rastas, such Ras Sam Brown, Ras Pidow, Bongo Shephan, Ras Ivi, and others, including several women. They travelled to such east coast cities as New York, Baltimore, Philadelphia, and Washington conducting educational workshops, giving cultural

10. Ras Ikael Tafari, PhD (sociologist) and Ras Historian, Rastafarian activist

performances (including Rasta drumming), and expounding the Nyabinghi traditions to their listeners. Prophet Gad (Vernon Carrington), founder of the Twelve Tribes of Israel, circulated among the various branches of this sect of Rastafari in Africa, New Zealand, England, the US, and elsewhere. The founder of the

Church of Haile Selassie is even more missionary minded in his approach, establishing and travelling among branches of the church in London, New York, Jamaica, Trinidad, and Belize (Homiak's 'From Yard to Nation' and Yawney's 'Rasta Mek a Trod' and 'Tell out King Rasta Doctrine around the World' provide further discussion of the tradition of 'trodding' among Rastas).

Adherents of Rastafari around the world have come to valorize Jamaica as the fountain head of their faith, and many who can afford the expense have gone there on personal missions/ pilgrimages to 'drink from the source'. Naturally, Jamaican Rastas and Rastas of Jamaican descent living abroad often return to the island to recharge themselves in the company of their local counterparts. Once they had embraced Rastafari, eastern Caribbean Rastas started making the trip to Jamaica to consult and ground themselves in the principles and practices of the movement. A good example of such missions is that of the venerable Vincentian Rasta, Ras Oba, who came to embrace a Rastafarian identity in New York in the mid-1970s after journeying through phases of black radical thought and politics. At a particularly difficult period of his life in the 1980s, he travelled from St. Vincent to Jamaica to participate in one of the periodic general gatherings of Rastas known as Nyabinghi. For a week, day and night, he listened to the speeches and biblical interpretations of revered Rastafarian elders; he smoked ganja and reasoned with Rastas from around the Caribbean and other parts of the world (including whites); and sang, chanted, and danced to Nyabinghi drumming into the early hours of the morning. For Oba this was the crowning event that confirmed his permanent identity as Rastafari. For similar reasons and with similar outcomes, Rastas from Africa have gone to Jamaica to experience Rastafari in its original environment. The earliest documented mission was that of two Tanzanian Rastas in 1986. Japanese Rastas are particularly famous for sojourning in Jamaica to study with long-established elders of the movement. In 1991, while researching Rastafarian motifs in a Jamaican craft market, I encountered a white South

African Rasta who had gone to Jamaica to savour the 'authentic' livity. In the imagination of Rastas around the world, Jamaica has therefore become a 'holy place' to which a pilgrimage is desirable in order to cement one's standing in Rastafari. Even children who have been born to Rastas in Shashamane, Ethiopia, look to Jamaica for their spiritual and cultural roots.

Though technically not missions, international assemblies, conferences, and workshops have become means of globalizing the message and experience of Rastafari and making international the network of relationships that prevails in the ethos of Rastafari. Beginning in Toronto in 1982 and convened in various locations since (Jamaica in 1983, Shashamane, Ethiopia, in 1992, Miami in 1994), these gatherings were conceived as venues for discussing pressing issues and forging solutions to persistent problems facing Rastafari. The Shashamane Assembly, celebrating the 100th birthday of Haile Selassie, was particularly noteworthy. The assemblies of the previous decades were all building to this historic date, when an international cohort of Rastas wended their way to the country and community that represented their greatest aspiration. The most significant outcome of this assembly was the rekindling of interest in the development of Shashamane as the Zion of Rastafari. The international Rastafarian community committed itself to the building of a permanent tabernacle (house of worship), and by 1998, the Shashamane Settlement Development Community Foundation was incorporated in Washington, DC, to provide support for the educational, housing, health, and recreational needs of the community of Rastas at Shashamane.

The creation of centralized institutions, the status of women in the movement, planning for and effecting repatriation, and the education of a growing number of neophytes around the world in the principles of Rastafari have all been debated and disputed at the gatherings of Rastafari. With the exception of financial support for Shashamane, not many practical or programmatic solutions have emerged from these deliberations. However, these conferences have served the social function of creating a sense of an international community, cementing global networks among adherents of Rastafari, and disseminating the 'orthodox' ethos of Rastafari that developed in Jamaica, especially among the Nyabinghi sect.

Attraction and adaptation

Two pressing questions that have emerged with the global spread of Rastafari are: 'why has Rastafari been so attractive to disparate people around the world?'; and 'how have different groups adopted and adapted it?'. Part of the attraction of Rastafari is that its message has resonated with the experiences and aspirations of many who have found themselves marginalized or alienated by the institutions and values of their societies. Rastafari's valourization of Africa and blackness provides African youths in the margins of post-colonial societies and black diasporic youths facing racial and cultural discrimination with a positive identity that can expunge psychologically their stigmatization. Furthermore, by dubbing Western societies and values as being those of Babylon, Rastafari provides disaffected people everywhere with a discursive stance from which to analyse and criticize the capitalist mode of production and the Western value of consumption. Thus, a Japanese Rasta can deploy the notion of Babylon to criticize Japanese and international capitalist economic and consumer culture. The tendency towards homogeneity, an intolerance of non-conformity, and the social inequality in Japan are magnified under the prism of the term 'Babylon'. In a similar fashion, young people wilting under the rigidity and authoritarianism of Cuba's socialist regime or indigenous Maoris subjected to economic and political domination by the descendants of European settlers immediately recognize the Babylonian forces framing their experiences and thwarting their dreams. But Rastafari not only provides them with an interpretive tool, it provides them with unmistakable symbols of resistance and defiance in the dreadlocks hairstyle and the smoking of marijuana.

In some cases, Rastafari's mystical relationship with nature and the supernatural and its emphasis on local folk values and community parallel and reawaken interest in other indigenous traditions. As anthropologist Marvin Sterling points out in *Babylon East*, Rastafari in Japan in one sense exemplifies a rediscovery and revitalization of Japanese folk identity that is located in rural areas in contrast with the modern Japanese identity shaped by urbanization and industrialization. Influenced by reggae and Rastafari, the Havasupai Indians of the Grand Canyon have come to regard Bob Marley as an incarnation of Crazy Horse, their esteemed hero who led a rebellion against white encroachment. Maori Rastas find proto-Rastafari manifestations in indigenous Maori values concerning nature, land use, and spirituality as well as in nineteenth century messianic movements resisting white domination and advocating self-determination. Their embrace of Rastafari provides them with a modern bridge to the re-appropriation of those indigenous values. For these Rastas in disparate places, Rastafari is not some foreign religion or culture that they are seeking to emulate. It is a form of mystical spirituality present to one degree or another in their indigenous cultures. Jamaican Rastafari is the contemporary impetus for the recognition and re-ignition of this mystical connection with the Creator and nature as taught in many folk cultures around the world.

The adoption or adaptation of Rastafari ranges from a simple parading of the trappings of the movement to a serious political, cultural, and spiritual engagement. For some, the cultivation of dreadlocks and donning of Rastafari-inspired wares do not go beyond aesthetics; for others they represent a statement of black identity comparable to the Afro hairstyle and wearing of African-inflected garb in the 1970s; for others (white youths in particular) they represent an anti-establishment impulse. Some adherents of Rastafari are more attuned to reggae music and Rastafari-inspired art. For them, Rastafari is more about the embrace of African and African diaspora culture. Political and social activism is how others find their way into the movement. Of course, the embrace of Rastafari as a spiritual and cultural way of life is also in vogue around the world. But even here, different aspects of Rastafari as developed in Jamaica are either inflected differently or rejected outright. For Rastas already living in Africa, repatriation is either de-emphasized or re-interpreted as an embracing of African culture and a form of African spirituality. In a similar vein, Brazilian Rastas harbour very little desire to return to Africa. Instead, they deem it a way of embracing African culture and identity. Obviously, it is not as easy for European or Asian Rastas to assert African identity. They tend to embrace InI consciousness and thus the universal dignity and equality of all humans. They also find appealing the Rastafarian emphasis on community and living in harmony with nature. Probably the greatest divergences occur with regard to the person and status of Haile Selassie. While his name is invoked by Rastas everywhere, not all accord him the divine status the Nyabinghis of Jamaica have conferred on him. The multi-ethnic, international 'house' of Rastafari called the Fulfilled Rasta is probably indicative of a widespread view of Haile Selassie held by disparate members of the movement. Selassie is an inspirational figure, probably a prophet, who calls his followers to a vision of social justice and harmony among the peoples of the world, but he is not divine.

From places with such names as Dungle, Back O' Wall, Ackee Walk, Trench Town, and Pinnacle in the margins of a colonial outpost of a dying British Empire, Rastafari has made the remarkable journey to become a religious and cultural force around the world. Emigration and travel first extended its reach beyond Jamaica; reggae music later became the vehicle through which its message was heard in the far reaches of the globe; and, eventually, Jamaican elders made 'trods' to emerging communities of Rastas to firm up their convictions, and Rastas from abroad made 'pilgrimages' to Jamaica to experience the genuine ethos of Rastafari. Like other religions with obscure origins, Rastafari has moved onto the world's stage, and is being embraced by many

Natural mystics

Since the 1960s, scholars and journalists have sought to come up with labels that classify Rastafari for their readers. 'Millenarianism', 'messianism', 'cargo cults', and 'nativism' were some of the terms used by early researchers. Since the 1970s, scholars have tended to highlight the political and cultural activism of the movement. Some scholars have referred to Rastafari as a new social movement, while others treat it as a new religious movement. Elsewhere (*Rastafari: From Outcasts to Culture Bearers*), I have indicated my preference for seeing Rastafari as a Revitalization Movement. In this light, it represents a post-colonial search for identity in the face of a Babylon culture that alienated and oppressed people of African descent and denigrated their culture. Fashioning this new identity entails a new worldview and the new cultural practices that I have discussed as Rastology and livity.

When asked about the character of their movement, Rastas themselves are likely to state that 'Rastafari is a way of life', indicating that it incorporates both social and spiritual aspects. In terms of its spiritual aspect, Rastafari holds to a kind of mysticism that narrows the distance between the divine and humans, as is evident in its concept of the 'I' as the divine essence in humans and in the professed ability to tap into the divine power ('earthforce') that suffuses the universe. Bob Marley makes reference to this in 'Natural Mystic', where he asserts that those who are attuned can perceive the 'natural mystical energy' moving through the atmosphere like radio waves. To affirm that the spirituality of Rastafari is not some new fantasy conjured up by deficient minds, Dennis Forsythe, in his book *Rastafari: For the Healing of the Nations*, characterizes Rastafari as the contemporary manifestation of the same mysticism found in ancient Africa (especially Egyptian religion) and later in Christian Gnosticism. The concept of 'InI', as the consciousness of one's divine self and one's communion with Jah, mirrors the identification of *atman* (self) with *Brahman* (the divine self) in Vedanta Hinduism, salvation as self-realization in Buddhism, and the quest for union with God in Sufi Islam, and some iterations of Christian mysticism. Unlike some mysticism, however, Rastafari is not world-rejecting. Rastafarian mysticism calls for humans to live in harmony with Jah, with one another, and with nature.

seeking to counter the forces that alienate them and to fashion lives of dignity and purpose. Ironically, the forces of globalization, travel, communication technology, and international commerce (especially for the music industry), have facilitated the spread of the ideas of a once marginalized community to others seeking refuge from some of the negative consequences of globalization.

Chapter 5
Kingmen, queens, and dawtas: gender issues in Rastafari

Women tend to dominate religious spaces in Jamaica. Historically, women in African-derived and Afro-Christian religious traditions have been just as likely as men to occupy positions of leadership and function as healers, preachers, and prophets. In the absence of numerical data, some even argue that women have outnumbered men as leaders in these traditions. Within the rank and file, women have enjoyed a sizeable numerical advantage. Though the leadership in Christian churches is mostly male, lay leaders and workers as well as the general membership are predominantly women. Most ministers will admit that without the organizational skills and the grassroots involvement of women the efficacy of church ministries would be greatly diminished if not impossible.

Running counter to this prevailing pattern, the Rastafarian ethos is dominated by men. While women were at Pinnacle, were observed in Rastafarian colours at early street meetings, and were arrested and tried along with their male counterparts by law enforcement agents, from the very beginning they were and have since remained a decided minority. Early observers noted that men significantly outnumbered women, and that women tended to be in the background while men presented themselves as the movers and mainstays of the movement. More recent ethnographic research and journalistic reports, though they lack hard numbers, have confirmed the minority presence and somewhat marginal influence of women in Rastafari. In the first 20 years of the movement, no elaborated gender roles apparently existed. Oral traditions claim that women were able to participate in rituals with men without any gender distinction. They smoked the chalice along with men and actively proclaimed the message of Rastafari. The patriarchy that now characterizes Rastafari can be traced to the House of Youth Black Faith and other radical Rastas of the late 1940s and 1950s. These Rastas developed a doctrine of female impurity, particularly during the menstrual cycle, and emphasized the threat of feminine seduction to a man's piety and moral rectitude. This discourse led to the marginalization of women in Rastafarian religious rituals and social interactions and became the bedrock of Rastafarian patriarchy.

While much of Rastafari is predicated on challenging structures of oppression and liberating people of African descent from Euro-centered ideology and social structures, the ethos and discourse of the movement traditionally privileges a kind of patriarchy in which women have been relegated to a second class status. The more conservative elements of the movement have adduced biblical teachings, especially Levitical codes, to elaborate an ideology of female inferiority. In the central rituals of the movement such as ganja smoking and Nyabinghi assemblies, women are frequently fringe actors if present at all. However, countervailing forces to patriarchy have always existed in the movement, and since the 1970s, Rastafarian women and men have actively challenged the ideology and practice of women's subordination.

Gender ideology and ethos

The examination of gender issues in Rastafari should begin with the recognition that Rastafari emerged as a movement focused on the redemption of the black male. It tacitly accepted the notion that, in the Americas, societies built upon slavery and its aftermath have robbed black men of their manhood, especially of their roles as heads of their households, providers of financial resources to their families, and leaders in their communities. For example, during the slave era, black men's ability to nurture their children was severely curtailed by their bondage; their female partners were often violated by white men with impunity; and whatever tenuous family life they were able to patch together often crumbled with the sale of family members. Some (including Rastas), who subscribe to the notion of black male emasculation and advocate for the restoration of black manhood, have even argued that, in slave and post-slave societies, those in power often deliberately elevated black women over black men, who were viewed as a threat to white supremacy. The restoration of black manhood is thus a primary goal of Rastafari. In this respect, Rastafari follows the same strategy as the Nation of Islam (founded in the US by Wallace D. Ford and Elijah Mohammad in the 1930s) which has placed a premium on rescuing African American males from their debilitation in American society and restoring them to a place of responsibility and honour in their family and community. As with the Nation of Islam, Rastafarian women are expected to embrace this project of redeeming black males and facilitate their psychological and social rehabilitation by submitting to their leadership.

The Jamaican cultural context in which Rastafari forged its gender perspectives subscribed to the notion of the father as the head of the family. However, in reality, fathers were often absent from or marginal to the day-to-day operation of the home. The sociological and anthropological literature indicates a chronic absenteeism of fathers in Jamaica, where over 70 per cent of children are born outside of marriage. And even where fathers may be present physically, many are absent emotionally. Most families are therefore matrifocal; that is, the axis around which they are organized is a strong woman – either mother or grandmother. In many cases where a patriarch is present, his headship is only titular. The real power broker in the family is the woman, though she may willingly ascribe family headship to her male partner if he is present. Rastafarian gender ideology and practices seek to restore men to their proper status and role as head of their women and families.

Ironically, the justification for Rastafarian patriarchy is grounded in biblical fundamentalism. As much as Rastafari claims to reject Jamaica's social norms as well as its folk and popular religions, it retains the biblical fundamentalism that is characteristic of Jamaica's religious culture in regards to the issue of gender. In fact, as the wider Jamaican public has evolved towards an ideology and practice of gender equity, many Rastas have promulgated an extreme patriarchy that relegates women to a position of inferiority. While the conventional Rastafarian approach to the Bible tends to appropriate and magnify its liberative themes while rejecting as interpolations passages that suggest submission and subordination to authoritarian forces, passages that enjoin women's subordination are uncritically embraced and deployed in order to enforce Rastafarian patriarchy. In this regard, Rastafarian discourse paints women as morally weak and susceptible to deception by evil forces. To buttress this idea, Rastas frequently cite the story of Eve's deception by the serpent in Genesis 3 and her subsequent inducing of Adam to partake of the forbidden fruit.

St Paul's teachings on gender relations provide Rastas with further evidence of women's moral frailty and the necessity for them to remain under male tutelage. In his interpretation of the Genesis story in I Timothy 2:11–15, Paul justifies his proscription against women's teaching men or exercising any form of authority over them by arguing that Eve, by bringing sin into the world, showed her (and women's) inability to lead. As he does in I Corinthians 14:34–35, he goes on here to insist that learning in silence, submission, and child-rearing are more appropriate roles for women. Though on occasions Paul seems to suggest gender equality (Galatians 3:27–8), he repeatedly calls on women and wives to submit to men and husbands (I Corinthians 11:5; Ephesians 5:23; Colossians 3:18). Since the I Corinthians 14 passage, especially, instructs the women not to ask questions in the congregation but to learn from their husbands at home, some Rastas have advocated that women cannot independently 'sight up' Rastafari (come to Rastafarian consciousness). They can only come to this realization through the tutelage of their 'kingmen'.

Traditional Rastafarian discourse imputes physical impurity to women in addition to their perceived moral and spiritual weakness. This Rastafarian position is informed by the Leviticus ceremonial law which declares a woman unclean for seven days during her menses (Leviticus 15:19–30), and probably by Jamaican folk ideas about menses as a contaminant. Rastas elevate this notion of impurity beyond their biblical or folk origins to a religious dogma that restricts a woman's activities during her menstruation period. The mildest form of such a practice simply prohibits women from handling men's food during these times. A stricter application calls for Rastafarian women to be in seclusion for seven days. The Bobo Dreads (Bobo Shanti) take the notion of menstrual impurity to the farthest extreme. For fear of contamination, women in their Bull Bay commune are not allowed to handle food meant for men at any time. What is more, menstrual seclusion starts the week before and continues the week after a woman's period, during which time a woman is confined to the care of other women in what is essentially a sick bay. This means that women only have sexual contact and social interaction with their menfolk about 12 days of each month.

Another area in which women's independence is circumscribed is their dress code. While men are free to wear whatever appeals to their sense of propriety or even their fancy, Rastafarian traditions prescribe that women's hair be covered, especially in public, and that their outfits should not reveal the contours of their bodies or any body part that may induce lust in men. Hence women are forbidden from wearing trousers (Deuteronomy 22:5), and are expected to wear long, flowing skirts and tops with sleeves that cover their arms. The rationale for this dress code is grounded in biblical, cultural, and social norms. First, it accords with the biblical call for modesty and simplicity (I Timothy 3:8–10). And since women's outfits are frequently made from African prints and in traditional African style, they indicate a re-appropriation of African heritage and identity. Augmented with the Rastafarian colours of red, green, and gold, women's apparel and accessories are unmistakable markers of Rastafarian identity. The propriety of Rastafarian women's clothing is also cast as resistance against Babylon's sexual objectification of women and the widespread flaunting of female sexuality through suggestive outfits. In this respect, both Rastafarian women and men are likely to attribute positive values to the prescribed dress code for women.

Rastafarian traditions also limit the sexual freedom and reproductive choices available to women. Sexual freedom and even sexual promiscuity are par for the course for some Rastafarian men. Having multiple sexual partners and 'baby mothers' simultaneously is quite commonplace for Rastafarian men (as it is for many Jamaican men). Bob Marley, the most internationally known Rasta and reggae superstar, is a prime example of the Rastafarian penchant for multiple partners. Though he was legally married to Rita Marley, Marley fathered children with between six and nine other women (not all claims of paternity have been substantiated), to say nothing of other sexual partners. Some Rastas embrace such behaviour, justifying it as a return to the African practice of polygamy, even though these relationships are not legally recognized. One could argue that this sanctifies the promiscuous sexual behaviour of Jamaican males. A Rastafarian woman, however, is expected to show unwavering fidelity to her 'kingman'. Women who violate this code of fidelity are likely to find themselves reviled as morally loose, shunned as pariahs, and may even become victims of physical violence from their men.

With regards to their reproductive choices, Rastafarian women are forbidden from using contraceptives and from aborting pregnancies. This restriction is informed by the biblical directive that humans should be 'fruitful and multiply, and fill the earth' (Genesis 1:28) and by a widespread Jamaican folk belief that a woman should 'have out her lot'. In addition, Rastafarian discourse paints abortion and contraceptives as part of white people's plot to destroy the black race. Furthermore, the artificial control of childbearing is seen as further evidence of Babylon's departure from the natural course designed by Jah. Women are therefore left with abstinence and the 'rhythm method' if they hope to limit the number of children they bear. Even this is not completely within their power, as any refusal of sexual intimacy with their men is likely to create conflict.

Probably the most egregious example of women's marginalization in Rastafari is their traditional exclusion from the ritual activities in which Rastafarian spirituality and sociality are cemented and celebrated. Central to the Rastafarian ethos, especially among Nyabinghi Rastas, is the frequent communal gatherings to smoke the ganja using the ritual pipe, often referred to as 'drawing the chalice', or to share large conical ganja cigars known as 'spliffs'. These smoking sessions are occasions for reasoning, the open-ended, free-flowing conversation in which Rastas exchange ideas and explore collective understanding of themselves and the structures and events of the world around them. While the historical evidence suggests that women joined men in ritual activities in the early days of Rasta, the dominant tradition, developed by House of Youth Black Faith and inherited by the Nyabinghi house, has been to exclude them from ritual smoking and reasoning. Nowadays, a post-menopausal woman with an impeccable reputation for 'livity' may be asked to prepare and light the chalice, but she will generally be excluded from the smoking and reasoning circle because she is regarded as lacking the spiritual and mental faculties to penetrate the depths of Rastafarian spirituality. In spite of opposition from the most conservative men, some Rastafarian women now form their own smoking and reasoning circles.

In a similar manner, the Nyabinghi Assemblies are dominated by male actors. Though women are allowed to attend, they are generally relegated to the background, while the central circle around the bonfire is occupied by men – dancing, smoking, and 'speechifying'. On occasions, women have been allowed to speak, but only through the intervention of respected male elders. The heartbeat of these gatherings is the ritual Nyabinghi drumming. However, this central Rastafarian ritual activity falls under the purview of men, and women are perceived as being incapable of creating the musical 'vibes' necessary to facilitate the reaching of the mystical heights the drumming is expected to induce. Despite their exclusion from ritual drumming, some Rastafarian women have endeavoured to master the playing of the drums. Making women marginal to the central ritual activities of Rastafari prohibits them from achieving equality with men and having the opportunity to contribute meaningfully to the formation and celebration of Rastafarian religiosity.

Countervailing forces

Given that the ideology and ethos of Rastafari tend to relegate women to a second class status, many question why women would embrace the movement at all. However, despite the culture of marginalization, there are countervailing forces in Rastafari that make it attractive to some women because they militate against extreme sexism. Before exploring these forces I must make two caveats concerning the research and writing of gender roles in Rastafari. The first is the sparsity of the research on Rastafari from the perspective of Rastafarian women. The subjects in most ethnographic and journalistic studies have been men, and therefore the voices of their female counterparts fail to surface in the results. This may be attributed to the fact that men have guarded the gateway to Rastafari and have denied researchers access to Rastafarian women. Notable exceptions have been Carole Yawney, who conducted research among Jamaican, Canadian, and South African Rastafarian women; Diane J. Austin, who investigated Rastafarian and Pentecostal women in Jamaica; and Loretta Collins, who studied Rastafarian women in Jamaica, Canada, and the United Kingdom. A related issue is that for the first four or five decades of the movement, Rastafarian women did not assert their voices in public discussion of Rastafari in general and gender issues in particular. Only since the 1970s have such Rastafarian women as Maureen Rowe, Barbara Makeda Lee, and Imani M. Tafari-Ama emerged to express their perspectives on Rastafari.

The second caveat is that much of the criticism of Rastafarian patriarchy assumes the normativity of Western feminist discourse. This is not to diminish or excuse Rastafarian patriarchy, but rather to point out that such criticism must take into consideration the inflection of local gender construction and social realities as well as the desires, wishes, and perspectives of local women. For example, with the endemic absenteeism of men from active roles in contributing economically to households and emotionally through supporting and nurturing their children, many Jamaican women may be less invested in articulating an ideology of gender equality that has no practical consequence in their daily lives. They may be more concerned with securing greater male responsibility. Some may even willingly cede headship to a 'good man' who will stick around to share the responsibilities of maintaining a household and raising a family.

Women embrace Rastafari for the characteristically positive personal, cultural, and social consciousness that it fosters in its adherents. Especially for women of African descent, whose self-image has been assaulted and denigrated by a history of European cultural imperialism, the Rastafarian tenet of InI consciousness confers a sense of inner divinity and personal dignity. Beyond this personal affirmation, Rastafarian positive appraisal of African history and culture is attractive to many women. Rastafari affirms their African physical features as well as their heritage and inspires them to cease pursuing the unattainable ideals of European beauty and cultural sophistication. For women of all ethnicities who embrace Rastafari, InI consciousness bestows an identity that elevates them beyond their sexuality, which is treated by Babylon as a quantifiable commodity. Female Rastas are also drawn to the Rastafarian critique of the social structures and institutions of the West in general and Jamaica's bourgeois society in particular. As a result of their marginalized socio-economic circumstances or their progressive political education, they readily subscribe to the stigmatization of these societies as Babylon, where power and privilege are to the benefit of the few while powerlessness and poverty remain the condition of the many. This kind of political consciousness informs their commitment to struggle for the upliftment of the 'downpressed' or downtrodden.

In Jamaica, Rastafarian men are more likely than the average male to be actively involved in nurturing children. This may soften the patriarchal and sexist ideology articulated by the movement. Unlike the normative relegation of child-rearing responsibilities exclusively to women in Jamaican culture, Rastafarian discourse emphasizes the responsibility of men in raising children in a caring and supportive environment. Rastas talk incessantly about the importance of raising the youths to develop positive self-esteem and values, thus counteracting the tendency of Babylon to create self-doubt and false values in children of African heritage. In general, Rastafarian males take this tenet of their faith seriously and seek to be present physically and emotionally in the lives of their children. Thus, it is not unusual to see Rastafarian men playing with their children and lovingly ministering to their needs. Some argue that this has emerged as a practical necessity, as Rastafarian women or Rastas' non-Rastafarian partners were often working while Rastafarian men were denied employment. In the formative decades of the movement, it was also highly likely that women would be estranged from their families for their embrace of Rastafari or association with Rastafarian men. Thus, if mothers were cut off from the network of female care-giving generally provided by other female family members, Rastafarian men would have to take up the responsibility of child-rearing out of sheer necessity.

Whatever its genesis, social commentators in Jamaica have hailed Rastafarian fathers as models for other Jamaican males. In Jamaican society, the nurturing of and caring for children are taken for granted as being the responsibility of women. Men's responsibility in the home is primarily, if not exclusively, relegated to providing financial support. In cases where women work outside the home, the responsibilities of childcare devolve to other women—grandmothers, aunts, older female children, or friends—but rarely to fathers, even if they are not gainfully employed. A man is likely to have his masculinity questioned if he is a primary care-giver to his children while his wife supports the family financially. He may become the object of teasing if his childcare responsibilities hinder him from joining his male friends in activities like watching sports, playing dominoes, or frequenting the local bar. In contrast with this acknowledged neglect of child-rearing responsibilities by men, Rastas have broken new and positive ground. In fact, where other Jamaican males view the care of children as ill-befitting a man, Rastas embrace it as part of the process of recovering their African manhood, denied them during slavery and by the current values governing the Babylon system.

While criticisms of Rastafari tend to focus on the articulated ideology, in some cases the lived experience belies the discursive stance. With respect to women in Rastafari, this has tended to be the case in at least two areas: female economic empowerment and women's roles in organizing Rastafarian activities beyond the confines of local Rastafarian groups. Social scientists have long observed that women who have independent access to economic resources are likely to improve their command of power in their homes and society. This holds true for Rastafarian women and non-Rastafarian partners of Rastafarian men. In many instances, women are the only members of a Rastafarian household who are gainfully employed on a regular basis. This disparity in male/female employment may have resulted from a female-friendly, service-oriented labour market, lower levels of education in

Jamaican men, discrimination against Rastafarians with dreadlocks, or the tendency of Rastafarian men to gravitate towards less lucrative artistic endeavours or subsistence agriculture. With the power of the purse, women who have paying jobs are likely to exert more influence over the men in their households and to have more freedom to operate independently within the movement and the society.

Since the 1980s, women have emerged as principal organizers of Rastafarian events. This new-found role correlates with the influx of middle class women into the movement, the global spread of Rastafari, and efforts to bring some level of centralization to this rather diffused movement. Makeda Patrica Silvera and Charmaine Masani Montague exemplify this convergence. Both were educated Rastafarian women living in Canada in the late 1970s when they founded the Rasta Cultural Workshop in Toronto in an effort to establish some level of coherence to Rastafarian activities in the city. They organized cultural and educational events to expose the Canadian public to the culture and spirituality of Rastafari and to debunk stereotypes of Rastafarian bizarreness and criminality promulgated by the Canadian media. Montague also played an essential role in organizing the First International Rastafarian Conference held in Toronto in 1982, the first of a series of gatherings motivated by a desire to bring unity and common purpose to the disparate, far-flung groups of Rastas around the world. Along with Carole Yawney, an expert in Rastafarian studies and an admirer and advocate of the movement, Montague facilitated the 'Voice of Thunder' dialogue in Toronto in 1984. This event brought the venerable Ras Boanerges along with two other Rastafarian elders from Jamaica to elaborate Rastafarian perspectives at a number of events in Toronto. Similarly, Rastafarian women in the United Kingdom, with Yawney's assistance, organized 'Rasta Focus' as part of a larger 'Caribbean Focus' in London in 1986 (see Figure 11).

In addition, other Rastafarian women organized a number of assemblies and various 'missions' between 1980 and 1994. Sister

11. Rasta women giving praise at a conference at UWI, Mona, 2010

Farika Berhane was the principal organizer of the second
International Rastafari Assembly held in Kingston, Jamaica, in
1983. Sister Desta Meghoo was instrumental in the 1992 assembly
in Shashamane to celebrate the centenary of Haile Selassie's birth.
She was also a key player in facilitating the Rastafari African
Family Gathering in Miami, Florida in 1994. Women were often
active in planning and participating in 'trods' or missions by
elders to inculcate the genuine Rastafari spirituality and livity in
local Rastafarian communities and to counter misinformation
about Rastafari around the world. For example, Sister Farika
Berhane, along with Jake Homiak, was responsible for organizing
the 'Rainbow Circle Throne Trod' of 1988 that took 26 Nyabinghi
Rastas, including four women, to several east coast cities in the
United States. Since the 1982 International Rastafari Assembly,
women have served as organizers, presenters, and discussants in a
number of international Rastafarian conferences. In addition to
the women mentioned above, Sister Marcia (Queen Mother Moses
Stewart) and Sister Ijahnya Christian are currently considered the
principal organizers of international Rastafarian gatherings (see
Yawney, 'Rasta Mek a Trod').

The most significant countervailing force against patriarchy in Rastafari has been the activism of women, demanding equality or refusing to abide by those practices they find exclusionary and inequitable. As with the assumption of organizational roles by Rastafarian women, the rise of activism came on the heels of the educated Jamaican middle class entering the movement in the 1970s. Educated women who embraced Rastafari were often influenced by black radicalism, especially the Black Power Movement, which spread rapidly on college and university campuses in the latter half of the 1960s. Drawn to Rastafarian Afro-centrism and its critique of the political, social, and cultural status quo in Jamaica, these women were initially more concerned with fashioning a new identity and supporting Rastafari against Babylon than with challenging the patriarchy of the movement. However, having equalled and even surpassed their male counterparts in educational institutions and the workplace, educated and independent Rastafarian women found the rabid patriarchy of Rastafarian elders chafing. In response to such concerns, Twelve Tribes surfaced to embody the less conservative leanings of newly minted, middle class Rastas. Unlike the rigid Nyabinghi traditions that had dominated Rastafari since the 1940s, Twelve Tribes gave its members, including women, a great deal of latitude in fashioning their individual lifestyle. In this 'house', women have been able to pursue Rastafarian livity without the harsher strictures that their sisters face in the Nyabinghi house and the house of Bobo Shanti.

Aside from the intervention of the Twelve Tribes house, Rastafarian women themselves began to interrogate and challenge their second class status in Rastafari. Judy Mowatt, one of the famed I-Threes backing singers for Bob Marley and a solo reggae artist, became a mouthpiece for female dignity and equality during the 1970s and 1980s, though she has since converted to evangelical Christianity. In her music and interviews, she celebrated the accomplishments of African women and voiced Rastafarian women's desire for liberation. Mowatt and other women, such as

Dawta Lois and dub poet Lillian Allen, argued that Rastafarian men can never achieve the freedom, equality, and justice they seek in society at large while perpetuating subordination of the women in their own movement. They insisted that equal status, opportunities, and treatment of women in Rastafari were fundamental to the aspiration of the movement as a whole. In addition, Rastafarian women began to shed light on gender issues in Rastafari through research and personal writings. In this respect, Barbara Blake Hannah (aka Barbara Makeda Lee), Maureen Rowe, and Imani M. Tafari-Ama were pioneers. Tafari-Ama was particularly invested in having men and women in the movement confront gender issues together. In her research, she gathered focus groups of Rastafarian men and women to discuss patriarchy and the place of women in the movement.

Both local and international events spurred discussion of Rastafarian gender ideology and practices. The most prominent local influence was the formation of the Sistren Theatre Collective (Tafari-Ama worked with this organization for a while) in the mid-1970s. This grassroots organization's main focus was the use of drama to explore such issues as sexism, domestic violence, and teen pregnancies in Jamaica. The international feminist movement of the 1970s, the rise of Womanism among African-American women, and the United Nations Decade of Women (1976–86) all contributed to Rastafarian women's growing consciousness of their marginalized position in the movement. Moreover, the international spread of Rastafari to societies like Canada, United States, and United Kingdom, where traditional patriarchy was already being questioned, brought into the movement women who were unwilling to surrender their independence. Rastafari also spread to indigenous communities, the Maori of New Zealand for instance, that traditionally accorded women greater status and public roles in social and religious matters.

By the 1980s, Rasta women were raising serious objections to their subordinate roles in Rastafari. In local and international gatherings, they repeatedly pressed for the recognition of their equality with men. Though traditional males often rebuff these requests, Rastafarian women have been joined by progressive men advocating for equality in Rastafari. Additionally, Rastafarian women have formed their own organizations, where they pursue their common interests and empower their communities. Notable organizations that provide opportunites for independent activities include King Alpha and Queen Omega's Theocracy Daughters, International Twelve, and Dawtas United Working Towards Africa (DAWTAS). Rastafarian women have also taken up leadership roles in more general Rastafarian organizations such as the Rastafari Youth Initiative. The 2006 documentary, *Roots Daughters: The Women of Rastafari*, highlights the Rastafarian women's contemporary challenge to gender biases in Rastafari. Both the attire and rhetoric of some women in the video suggest that they are willing to be transgressive of conservative directives about their behaviour. Some women appear wearing trousers or sleeveless dresses; others, instead of covering their heads, have their flowing locks on full display. Even more importantly, several women openly express their opposition to the gendered ideology and practices of Rastafari and call for equal participation of Rastafarian women in playing the drums, drawing the chalice, and reasoning with men.

Though the use of such terms of endearment as empress, queen, and dawta (daughter) to refer to Rastafarian women are believed to elevate the status of women, they re-inscribe the subordinate status of women and their dependence on their men folk. The empress is always attached to the emperor, the queen is always subjected to the king (kingman), and dawta is a generic term for women, regardless of age, under the tutelage of a husband or father. However, contemporary Rastafarian women are drawing inspiration from female icons of Rastafari to assert their dignity and pursue equal status in the movement. In this respect, Empress Menen (Queen Omega), the stately and dignified wife of Haile Selassie, and the legendary Queen Nyabinghi have become symbols of women's agency to resist domination from without or within.

Chapter 6
'The head cornerstone': Rastafari and Caribbean culture

In 'Ride Natty Ride', Bob Marley declared, 'But the stone that the builder refuse [sic] shall be the head cornerstone.' In these words, Marley is drawing on a biblical reference to the proverbial and prophetic rejected stone that eventually emerged as the cornerstone of the building. The statement first appeared in Psalm 111:18, and the New Testament writers consistently applied it to Jesus, rejected by his own people but nevertheless made the cornerstone or capstone of the church, the new people of God (Matthew 21:42, Mark 12:10, Luke 20:17, Acts 4:11, and I Peter 2:7). In *Ride Natty Ride*, Marley gives these words an apocalyptic slant. The song is a narrative of reversal and redemption, in which the once despised and rejected (Rastas) emerge as the victors while the oppressors are vanquished by becoming the victims of a raging conflagration. Though Marley's language is apocalyptic, it is equally valid to applying the metaphor of the rejected stone becoming the cornerstone to the trajectory of Rastafari, from being a despised and rejected subculture to being the most creative and central element of Caribbean culture. From these men and women considered eccentrics and social misfits, denizened in 'camps' and communes in the urban ghettos and on the periphery of Kingston, came an efflorescence of creativity that influenced Jamaican and Caribbean culture from the 1950s onwards. Their creative energy radically reshaped Jamaica's cultural landscape, giving Jamaica and the Caribbean an indigenous musical and artistic tradition recognized around the world. Once considered pariahs, lunatics, and trouble-makers, by the 1970s Rastas were being celebrated as a potent cultural force.

Nyabinghi drumming, Rastafarian consciousness, and reggae music

The transition of Rastafari from the margins of Jamaican culture to its centre and to a prominent presence on the world's stage is most evident in its contribution to music. At the time of Rastafari's emergence, an array of indigenous musical traditions existed in Jamaica. The Maroons (a community of escapées from enslavement), having been ensconced in their semi-autonomous enclaves since the 1700s, maintained much of their African musical traditions. Folk religious traditions, such as Revival Zion, Pocomania, Convince Cult, and Kumina, all had African-derived drumming traditions that accompanied congregational singing and spirit-possession rites. A number of African-derived folk performances, parades, or festivals were also part of the musical fabric. These included Burru, Brukins, Gere, Gumbay, Jonkunu, and Dinki Mini. Added to the folk traditions were a variety of secular and religious genres from Great Britain and the United States. With the migration of Jamaicans throughout the Americas and the advent of radio, influences from Latin music, Trinidadian calypso, and American popular music also made their way to Jamaica.

By the time West Kingston became the favourite haunt of Rastas, some of these local and international musical genres were meeting and influencing one another in slums that had been established there by migrants from rural areas. Influenced mainly by Burru, Kumina, and Revival drumming, Rastas developed their own ritual music style called Nyabinghi drumming by the 1950s. Burru proved to have the most decisive influence on the music of Rastafari. Burru was a traditional drumming style utilized in the fields during the time of slavery to keep the rhythm of work at a steady pace and thus to improve productivity. During slavery and

Marketing of reggae and Rastafari

Reggae Sunsplash and Reggae Sumfest exemplify the commodifying and marketing of reggae and Rastafari. Started in Montego in 1978, Reggae Sunsplash quickly became the largest reggae music festival in the world, attracting thousands of visitors to the island from as far away as Japan, and providing an economic boost to Jamaica's tourism during the slow July–August period. Since 1984, travelling Reggae Sunsplash festivals have been held every summer around the world. While the Sunsplash in Jamaica was a boon for the tourist industry, the organizers, Synergy Productions, experienced recurring financial difficulties, leading to its discontinuation in 1998. By then it had been replaced by Reggae Sumfest, started in 1993, as the major attraction for reggae lovers to travel to Jamaica to revel in the music as well as the sea and sun. Though efforts have been made to revive Reggae Sunsplash in Jamaica since 2006, Reggae Sumfest has remained the prime reggae festival for visitors and entertainers alike.

after emancipation, Burru drummers often organized themselves into troupes that marched through communities from Christmas to the New Year displaying their music artistry and singing ditties that parodied and criticized community members for their rumoured moral failings. Rastas encountered Burru drumming in the West Kingston slums and were attracted to it because they considered it a pure African musical tradition that survived in Jamaica. A number of Rastas in the Trench Town and Dungle areas of West Kingston adopted Burru drumming and became celebrated local virtuosos. Among these were: Watto King, a drum maker and burru player who converted to Rastafari; Brother Philmore Alvaranga, who became a member of Count Ossie's band and the initial financial backer of the group; Ras Michael, who later formed the band Ras Michael and the Sons of Negus; Brother

John and Brother Rubba, who were noted for their aggressive drumming styles; and others such as Pa-Ashanti from Foreshore Road, Brother Skipper, and Brother Joe. Count Ossie (Oswald Williams), who learned his craft from a Burru man named Brother Job and from Brother Watto King, has become the most celebrated master drummer for adopting the drumming style of Burru and their three-drum set called the 'akete'. With some experimentation, Ossie and his associates transformed Burru into Rastafarian ritual music and popularized it by playing at small and large Rastafarian gatherings called 'groundings' or 'groundations' in Kingston and its periphery.

As Jamaican popular music evolved from the 1950s onwards, both the rhythmic quality of the music and the message of the lyrics were increasingly influenced by Rastafari. Mento, which thrived from the 1930s to 1950s, can be considered the first popular music of modern Jamaica. It first developed as a rural folk genre that was played at community functions and celebrations such as parades, festivals, and Christmas and New Year parties. Mento's instrumentation was provided by banjo, acoustic guitar, small hand drums, rhumba box (mbira), and fife. The rhythm was accented on the afterbeat. The lyrics were dominated by topical concerns and were often slanted towards the treatment of sex, relationship issues, and salacious rumours through the use double or multiple entendres. By the mid-1950s, mento players were entertaining tourists in the developing tourist areas along Jamaica's north coast. They were also making appearances in Kingston's fancy clubs which were frequented by Jamaica's upper and middle classes. The rise of the recording industry in Jamaica, especially through the pioneering work of Stanley Motta, contributed to the popularity of the genre in the 1950s.

The Jamaican independence movement, which started in the 1930s and culminated with independence from Great Britain in 1962, also fuelled a drive for cultural independence that found musical expression in 'ska' in the late 1950s and early 1960s.

The earliest recordings in the ska genre, sometimes called 'bluebeat', were essentially covers of rhythm and blues hits from the United States, but done with Jamaican accents and musical sensibilities. These recordings were stimulated by the need to make up for the slump in the number of rhythm and blues records available to local sound systems because the American music scene had been taken over by the rock and roll craze. However, by the early 1960s cultural nationalists and pioneering producers such as Prince Buster and Clement 'Coxsone' Dodd were experimenting with combining local elements, especially the afterbeat accent of mento, with African-American influences to give ska a distinctive Jamaican flavour. The Skatalites that provided the instrumental accompaniment to the majority of ska recordings between 1963 and 1966 epitomized the classic ska sound with its galloping bass, breezily fast rhythms, 'chopping' staccatos, and jazzy horn accents.

By 1966, ska was superseded by rock steady, which was characterized by a dramatic slowing down of the tempo and the foregrounding of the drum and bass. Commentators have suggested that rock steady reflected the social stress palpable in the society at the time. The slow pulsating rhythms mirrored the seething social tensions born of the failed promise of political independence to end inequities and to bring peace and prosperity to all. The rock steady dance, described as 'renting a tile', found the dancer marking time in the same spot as if riveted there by some internal tension that should be massaged delicately and released slowly to prevent it from exploding. Interestingly, the subject that received most attention in the lyrics of rock steady songs was the rude boy phenomenon. Rude boys were urban outlaws who challenged the inequities of society and took an attitude of defiance towards law enforcement authorities. The rude boys adopted the anti-establishment stance of Rastafari, but not necessarily its spirituality. As a kind of urban cowboy, rude boys lived and died by guns and 'ratchets' (a kind of knife).

By the late 1960s, the maturing and blending of previous musical forms culminated in reggae. Musically, reggae speeds up the tempo of rock steady, features a prominent melodic bass line, and adds a half tone to the characteristic afterbeat of ska. Of course, Jamaican musicians continued to be influenced by their counterparts abroad. The musical and political ferment in the United States in the 1950s often provided inspiration for Jamaican musicians, and artists such as Curtis Mayfield, Marvin Gaye, and Stevie Wonder were very influential (Wailers' 'One Love' was modelled after Mayfield's 'People Get Ready'). Even rock and roll provided musical inspiration. As reggae gained international recognition in the 1970s, rock guitar runs ('flourishes') started to appear in reggae, especially in the music of Bob Marley and the Wailers and the Third World Band. Lyrically, the topical commentary that debuted in ska and graduated to serious social criticism in rock steady became even more prominent in reggae.

During the mento era, Rastafari took its first steps in making its presence felt in local popular music. This is exemplified in a calypso-inflected mento recording by Lord Lebby and accompanied by the Jamaican Calypsonians in the 1950s. Entitled 'Ethiopia', the song not only captures the sentiments of Rastas about Ethiopia and their longing to repatriate there, but it also contains elements of Nyabinghi drumming, especially the playful flourishes of the peta. By the time the 1960s rolled around, musicians of Rastafarian persuasion were making their marks on the emerging popular music. Don Drummond and Count Ossie were stand-outs among their peers.

Don Drummond is still celebrated as one of Jamaica's musical geniuses and its greatest trombonist. He received his education at Alpha Boys schools that became famous for providing at-risk boys with excellent music training. Drummond was a member and sometimes leader of the legendary Skatalites, which have been credited with creating and disseminating the characteristic ska sound. As an adherent of Rastafari and an ardent black nationalist,

Drummond brought his cultural sensibilities and Rastafarian vision to his artistic craft. Such instrumental compositions as 'Man in the Street', 'Confucius', 'Eastern Standard Time', The Reburial [of Marcus Garvey], 'Roll Sweet Don', and 'Don Cosmic' are believed to reflect the mysticism and sense of dread that pervade Rastafari. Unfortunately, Drummond suffered from mental illness that led to his conviction for taking the life of his girlfriend, Anita Mahfood, in 1965. He was committed to Jamaica's infamous Bellevue Mental Asylum, where he died in 1969 at the young age of 37.

The role of Count Ossie in inserting Rastafari into the evolving popular music was even more direct and far-reaching. In 1960, Ossie was commissioned by Prince Buster to arrange 'Oh Carolina' and accompanied the Folkes Brothers on its recording. A song lamenting the loss of a lover, 'Oh Carolina' became the first local hit of the ska era and gained popularity abroad, especially in the United Kingdom. Though the lyrics of the song expressed no Rastafarian sentiments, its accompaniment was heavy with Nyabinghi drumming provided by Ossie and his drum troupe. After 'Oh Carolina', Ossie and his band, the Mystic Revelation of Rastafari, had a productive performing and recording career well into the 1970s, releasing two critically acclaimed albums, *Groundation* in 1973 and *Tales of Mozambique* in 1975. Since his death in 1976, collections of his recordings have been published as *Man from Higher Heights* in 1983 and *Remembering Count Ossie: A Rasta Reggae Legend* in 1996.

Ossie's importance lies less in his own performances and recording career and more in his role in introducing Rastafarian music to the 1960s generation of musicians who contributed to the development of Jamaica's musical traditions. After his success with 'Oh Carolina', Ossie's East Kingston Rastafarian camp became a gathering place for many local musicians, including members of the Skatalites. There, they partook of the 'holy herb', listened to Rastafarian philosophizing (reasoning), and, most importantly, participated in extended jam sessions with Ossie and other

Rastafarian drummers. The end result was that these musicians not only learned the nuances of Nyabinghi drumming, but also went on to simulate it on conventional instruments.

From there the incorporation of Rastafarian rhythms into popular music followed almost inevitably. The Nyabinghi bass drum was imitated by the bass guitar and the bass drum of the trap set; the 'funde' syncopation was reproduced in the 'skeng-ay' rhythms on the keyboard and the rhythm guitar; and 'peta' improvizations found their way into the phrasings of the lead guitar. Rastafarian chants were often arranged and presented as reggae, often accompanied by the unadulterated Nyabinghi drumming style. The Wailers' repertoire includes such chants as 'The Lion of Judah', 'So Long Rastafari Call You', 'Zion Train', and 'Babylon Throne Gone Down'. The lyrics and music of other Wailers' hits such as '400 Years' (Peter Tosh), 'Get Up Stand Up', and 'Forever Loving Jah' were influenced by chants they had heard at grounding ceremonies. The Wailers were not the only ones recording and performing Rastafarian chants as reggae. The Melodians recorded 'Rivers of Babylon', later made world famous by Boney M, and Steel Pulse recorded 'Nyabinghi Voyage'. Rastafarian chants remain sources of reggae songs as exemplified by the recording of 'No Night in Zion' in 1997 and 2001 by Culture and Luciano respectively.

Reggae not only incorporated Nyabinghi rhythms and appropriated Rastafarian chants, but, from the late 1960s to the 1970s, it suffused its social criticism of Jamaican society with the language, motifs, and point of view of Rastafari. The very titles of popular hits from the period tell the story: 'Israelites' by Desmond Decker and the Aces, 'Better Must Come' by Delroy Wilson, 'Jah Kingdom Gone to Waste' by Ernie Smith, 'War inna Babylon' by Max Romeo, 'Marcus Garvey Words Come the Past' by Burning Spear, and 'Babylon System' and 'Crazy Baldheads' by the Wailers. Though social criticism was not the only topic of reggae lyrics, unrelenting commentary on the perceived corruption and oppressiveness of local and international institutions, through the lens of Rastafari, was a dominant theme.

Marley's death in 1981 seemed to signal the end of the classic era of reggae, as dancehall ('deejay', 'ragga') stormed onto the Jamaican music scene in the early 1980s and remained there ever since. Characterized by musical minimalism, in which drum and bass submerge most of the melodic line, and by lyrics that privilege braggadocio, gun violence, and explicit sexual content, dancehall sidelined the Rastafarian philosophy in Jamaica's popular music. However, reggae artists of Rastafarian persuasion continue to make music that reflects their social and cultural consciousness. Since the mid 1990s, new artists such as Anthony B, Capleton, Garnett Silk, Luciano, Buju Banton, and many others, have worked to restore Rastafarian spirituality and social consciousness to a place of centrality both in the dancehall genre and classic reggae.

Rastafarian iconography and visual culture

The emergence of Rastafari in the 1930s coincided with an upsurge of national consciousness in Jamaica. Seeking to displace the colonial power structure of the waning British Empire, the nationalists aimed to gain power and social recognition through advocating voting rights and, eventually Jamaica's political independence from Great Britain; this was achieved in 1962. One element of the nascent nationalism of the 1920s and 1930s was the emergence of a local arts movement whose acknowledged founder was Edna Manley, an Anglo-Jamaican sculptor who was the wife of Norman Manley, one of the architects of trade unionism in Jamaica and Jamaica's independence movement. While Norman was busy on the political front fashioning a nationalist movement that agitated for universal adult suffrage, self-government, and eventually independence, Edna was creating images and training artists (eventually founding the Jamaica School of Arts in the 1940s—now the Edna Manley School of

Visual and Performing Arts) that reflected the emerging political and cultural consciousness. Her most iconic sculpture of the period, *Negro Aroused* (see Figure 12), is a half image of an unmistakably black man gazing upward, symbolizing an awakened consciousness and a steely determination to participate in the creation of a new Jamaica that recognizes and celebrates the African heritage of most of its people.

In the earliest days of the Jamaican art movement, Rastafari seemed to have escaped the gaze of both classically trained and intuitive (untrained) artists. However, artists gradually came to recognize Rastafari as a subject, then to show a growing sympathy for the Rastafarian perspective, and eventually to deploy Rastafarian ideas and motifs to express both African nationalism and Jamaican folk consciousness. Artistic attention to Rastafari increased from the 1950s to the 1980s as the negativity imputed to the movement lessened and as it became associated with social and cultural change in the newly independent nation.

Edna Manley herself may have been responsible for the discovery of Rastafari as a subject of art. Her little-known 1940 drawing, entitled *Dispossessed*, depicts what appears to be a Rasta man, capturing the sense of alienation and marginalization that characterized Rastafari at that time. Other Jamaican artists and foreign artists domiciled in Jamaica followed Edna Manley's lead in turning their artistic gaze to Rastafari. In 1955, David Miller, Sr. sculpted *Rasta: Don't Touch I*, depicting a dreadlocked Rasta sitting on a bench with one of his hands in a defensive position. According to art historian Veerle Poupeye, this piece grew out of the artist's personal experience of being drawn to the novelty of the dreadlocks hairstyle and wanting to touch it to get a feel of its texture. The piece captures the typical Rastafarian response of forbidding the curious from desecrating his locks. At about the same time as Miller, the prolific Jamaican painter Carl Abrahams began to show Rastafarian influences in his painting *Last Supper* (1955).

12. *Negro Aroused* by Edna Manley

Though not very distinct, some of the images in the paintings are recognizably black (contrary to the white figures in European depictions of the Last Supper), suggestive of Rastas. This influence continues in rather submerged fashion in *The Thirteen Disciples* (1975), but became explicit in two works in 1978, both entitled *Three Rastas*. In 1980, Koren der Harootian, an Armenian artist who lived in Jamaica for extended periods, painted *Homage to Rasta*. Though an expatriate, Harootian by the very title of this work recognizes Rastafari with a certain respect and deference. Eventually, Edna Manley returned to the subject of Rastafari in 1980 giving it an unmistakably sympathetic portrayal in *The Voice*. This sculpted head of a Rasta suggests that Rastafari had become the voice of the people, especially the dispossessed.

Even before *The Voice*, Jamaican artists such as Seya Parboosingh and Osmond Watson were bringing strong and distinctive Rastafarian sensibilities to their work, even though they themselves were not Rastas. Parboosingh's sympathies are abundantly evident in *Confrontation* and *Ras Smoke I*, painted in 1972 and *Rasta with Abeng*, painted in 1973. These works purposefully linked Rastas to the historic tradition of resistance of the dominant British colonial power in Jamaica. In many of Watson's works, Rastafarian influence is even more far-reaching. Watson not only uses Rastafari to express his African/black consciousness, but he has also grafted elements of Rastafari into his very persona, which is often the subject of his paintings. As Veerle Poupeye points out in her book, *Caribbean Art*, Watson's famous *Peace and Love*—a classic Rastafarian greeting—is an autobiographical portrait of himself utilizing a 'Rastafarianized' depiction of Christ. His *Rainbow Triptych*, done in the style of iconographic stained glass paintings, doubles as a portrait of Jesus, Mary, and the baby Jesus as well as of Watson, his wife, and their child. Such works as *Hymn for Jah*, *Ecce Homo*, and *The Mystic* bear similar interpretations. They all show Watson's characteristic merging of the spiritual and the autobiographical, utilizing Rastafarian perspectives. His works boldly assert the divinity of the individual, which is a foundational tenet of Rastafari.

Eventually, artists of Rastafarian persuasion rose to prominence in Jamaica and beyond. In fact, when compared to people of other religious persuasions, a relatively high number of Rastas are represented in the arts, as they are in music. This is probably an outgrowth of their desire to escape what they consider the exploitation of their labour in the formal economy. Furthermore, in the early decades of the movement, many talented persons lost their jobs when they embraced Rastafari, especially where such embrace was signalled by adopting the dreadlocks hairstyle. The result was that many turned to the making of art and crafts that they could sell in the informal economy, particularly in tourist zones. Also of significance is the fact that Rastafari itself is a religious tradition that is rich in strong visual imageries and powerful symbols, such as dreadlocks, lions, and the colours red, green, and gold. These imageries and symbols find artistic representations in the icons and emblems of the movement. So it is not surprising that Rastafarian artists would bring their sensibilities and convictions to the artistic endeavour.

A number of intuitive (self-taught) Rastafarian artists have risen to prominence in Jamaica and their works are collected and exhibited abroad. Among them are Ras Dizzy, Ras Daniel Heartman, Everald Brown, and Albert Artwell. Apart from the use of colours, Rastafarian themes are mostly subdued in the paintings of the eccentric and peripatetic Ras Dizzy. He focuses on themes drawn from the local environment and culture and shows a predilection for cowboy themes because of his love of Westerns and for self-portraits of himself as a jockey—an occupation in which he once engaged. Today, his colourful and symbolic paintings appear in several galleries including the National Gallery of Jamaica.

The art of Ras Daniel Heartman, Everald Brown, and Albert Artwell deals more explicitly with Rastafarian themes. Working with pencil drawings, Heartman has produced some of the most iconic representations of Rastafarian identity and philosophy. His early works may be characterized as iconographic theologizing or philosophizing. For example, to convey Rastas' conviction that they possess the poise, courage, confidence, and power of the lion, Heartman riffs on the Bible story of Daniel in the lion's den to produce a self-portrait, entitled *Daniel in the Lion's Den*, in which his face is surrounded by multiple lions emerging from his dreadlocks and his beard. Of course, he is playing on his own first name, Daniel, while evoking Rastas' belief in their own lion-heartedness. *Not Far Away*, probably his most well-known piece, performs a similar artistic feat. The foreground of the piece is dominated by a self-portrait in which Heartman's cascading locks merge with the mane of the lion standing before him. Both Heartman and the lion have a faraway gaze that is presumably focused on the palace in the background (seen through the lion's legs) guarded by another lion. Obviously this is an artistic representation of Ethiopia/Africa as the spiritual/ cultural home of Rastas and of their longing to return to what they consider their ancestral homeland. For good measure, Heartman places an outline of a ganja (marijuana) plant somewhere between the foreground and background images, symbolizing the role of the holy herb in facilitating the rediscovery of Rastas' African and divine identity. *An Ancient Olympian*, which depicts Heartman wrestling and merging his physical form with that of a lion, returns to the theme of Rastas' leonine nature, but this time riffing on Roman gladiatorial sports. Even when the lion is absent, Heartman's works, even his portrait of children including his own son (*Prince Emmanuel, Prince Mani, Rasta Boy*, for example), convey the sense of confidence, determination, dignity, and assertive masculinity that is characteristic of Rastafarian male identity. In his later years (he died in Tanzania in 1989), Heartman's works took a decidedly more mystical and symbolic turn. This turn is evident in *Mystic Presence, Immortality*, and a 1985 untitled work. By this time he was deep into Egyptian mysticism, hieroglyphics, and iconography, and these are reflected in his work.

Everald Brown's works abound with Rastafarian symbolisms, evident in the colours used and the combination of images. His *Ethiopian Apple*, obviously alluding to the mythical 'apple' of the Garden of Eden, depicts an 'otaheite' apple tree (a local Jamaican fruit tree) superimposed on a priestly figure who is surrounded by three drummers. First, both the figures and the background are suffused with the colours red, green, and gold. Second, by replacing otaheite with Ethiopia, the artist invokes the Rastafarian belief in Ethiopia as the ancestral home of Rastas, the source of their spiritual inspiration, and as Zion, the future home to which they aspire to return. Third, the superimposition of the tree upon the priestly figure highlights the Rastafarian assertion of being grounded in creation (nature). This is the same kind of organic relationship between humans and the environment captured in Christopher Gonzalez's sculpture of Bob Marley, whose lower extremities seem to emerge from the ground as a tree trunk. This cosmic oneness and Rastafarian symbolism pervade other works by Brown, for example *Mystic Hills*, *Stone Man*, *Tree of Jessie*, and *Nyabinghi Hour*.

Influenced by Ethiopian iconographic painting that arranges images vertically, Albert Artwell seeks to convey unmistakable Rastafarian messages in his paintings. He does this clearly in his *Judgment Day*, which is an apocalyptic vision of the downfall of Babylon—Western oppressive societies. Done in Rastafarian colours, the painting consists of three layers of people. The upper layer is obviously heaven where angel-like Rastas are happily according praise to the divine, kingly being, who straddles the upper and middle layer. The middle layer is obviously earth and consists of people dressed in black, holding some kind of book, and gesturing to the divine, kingly being who is presumably their judge. The bottom layer shows people being tormented by other figures dressed in red. It is in this hell that the only obviously white person appears in the picture.

These are just a sampling of Rastafarian artists and their works. As Rastafari has spread throughout the Caribbean and the world, it has produced Rastafarian artists everywhere and has influenced the art of non-Rastas wherever it has embedded itself. But beyond its influence on the visual arts (painting and sculture), Rastafari has made imprints on the wider visual culture of Jamaica and the Caribbean. Rastafarian colours and symbols are used copiously in the graphic arts. Advertising and product marketing make frequent use of these symbols to sell everything from records to concerts, to rum, to tourism (see Figure 13). Since the 1970s, Rastafarian symbols have become inextricably linked to Jamaican and Caribbean folk culture. Hence, items marketed to tourists as emblems of Jamaican culture abound with Rastafarian motifs exceeding all other motifs combined. Jamaican craft markets and roadside stalls, especially in tourist areas, offer a dazzling array of art and craft abounding in Rastafarian colours and motifs: wood carvings, paintings, t-shirts, skirts, hats, handbags, necklaces, and earrings. As should be expected, the image that occurs most frequently is the image of Bob Marley, though he is getting some competition these days from Jamaican celebrity sprinter, Usain Bolt. Beyond Jamaica, Rastafari has become a generic representation of the Caribbean for the tourist trade. Even Caribbean countries not known to have strong Rastafarian communities (the Bahamas, Dominican Republic, and Puerto Rico) make use of Rastafarian images and colours to sell their t-shirts to tourists.

While I have confined my discussion to Rastafarian influence on music and visual arts, the literary field and performance arts have also drawn inspiration from the movement's valourization of African and vernacular culture. Dub poetry, closely associated with reggae and often recited to the accompaniment of reggae rhythms, employs the vocabulary, speech style, and metaphors characteristic of Rastafarian language. Among the internationally recognized dub poets are Michael Smith, Oku Onuora, and Mutabaruka, all of whom are also renowned proponents of Rastafari. More generally, Jamaican and other Caribbean poets, who are not Rastas, often reflect the cadences of Rastafarian speech and the concerns of the Rastafarian worldview in their work. Fiction writers have increasingly incorporated Rastafari as a subject in their works or followed Rastafari and reggae in

13. Commodification: head wares in Rastafarian colours of red, gold, and green

privileging the local voice and concerns of the people. Roger Mais's *Brotherman* initiated this trend in 1954, followed by Orlando Patterson's *The Children of Sisyphus* in 1965. Since then, as Kwame Dawes has argued in *Natural Mysticism: Towards a Reggae Aesthetic in Caribbean Writing*, Rastafari and reggae have provided Anglophone Caribbean writers with a distinctive voice that has liberated them from mimicking the aesthetics of British literature. Bob Marley is certainly right. The rejected and maligned Rastafari has become the cornerstone of Caribbean cultural production, whether in music, art, or literature.

Further reading

Adams, Norman (Jah Blue), *A Historical Report: The Rastafari Movement in England* (London: GWA Works, 2002).

Ahkell, Jah, *Rasta: Emperor Haile Selassie and the Rastafarians* (Chicago, IL: Research Associates School Times, 1999).

Augier, Roy and Veronica Salter (eds.), *Rastafari: The Reports* (Kingston, Jamaica: Caribbean Quarterly, University of the West Indies, 2010).

Barnett, Michael (ed.), *Rastafari in the New Millennium: A Rastafari Reader*, (Syracuse, NY: Syracuse University Press, 2012).

Barrett, Leonard E., *The Rastafarians: Sounds of Cultural Dissonance*, revised edn (Boston, MA: Beacon Press, 1988).

Bender, Wolfgang, *Rastafarian Art of Jamaica* (St Charles, IL: Warwick Publishing, 2007).

Boxhill, Ian (ed.), *The Globalization of Rastafari* (Kingston, Jamaica: Arawak Publications, 2008).

Brown, John, *Shades of Grey: Police–West Indian Relations in Handsworth* (Birmingham: Cranfield Police Studies, 1977).

Campbell, Horace, *Rasta and Resistance: From Marcus Garvey to Walter Rodney* (Trenton, NJ: African World Press, 1987).

Caribbean Quarterly, *Rastafari: A Monograph* (Kingston, Jamaica: Caribbean Quarterly, University of the West Indies, 1985).

Cashmore, Ernest, *Rastaman: The Rastafarian Movement in England* (London: George Allen & Unwin, 1983).

Chevannes, Barry, *Rastafari: Roots and Ideology* (Syracuse, NY: Syracuse University Press, 1994).

Collins, Loretta, 'Daughters of Jah: The Impact of Rastafarian Womanhood in the Caribbean, the United States, Britain, and

Canada', in Hemchand Gossai and Nathaniel Samual Murrell (eds.), *Religion, Culture, and Tradition in the Caribbean* (New York: St. Martin's Press, 2000).

Colman, George D., *Oba's Story: Rastafari, Purification and Power* (Trenton, NJ: Africa World Press, 2005).

Davis, Stephen and Peter Simon, *Reggae Bloodlines: In Search of the Music and Culture of Jamaica* (Garden City, NY: Anchor, 1977).

Dawes, Kwame, *Natural Mysticism: Towards a New Reggae Aesthetics* (Leeds: Peepal Tree, 1999).

Edmonds, Ennis B., *Rastafari: From Outcasts to Culture Bearers* (New York: Oxford University Press, 2003).

Forsythe, Dennis, *Rastafari: For the Healing of the Nation* (Brooklyn, NY: One Drop Books, 1996).

Hansing, Katrin, *Rasta, Race and Revolution: The Emergence and Development of Rastafari Movement in Socialist Cuba* (Berlin: LIT VERLAG, 2006).

Henzell, Perry (writer and director) and Rhone, Trevor D. (co-writer), *The Harder They Come* (New World Pictures, 1972).

Homiak, John P., 'From Yard to Nation: Rastafari and the Politics of Eldership at Home and Abroad', in Manfred Kremser (ed.), *Ay Bōbō, 3: Rastafari (Afro-Caribbean Cults: Resistance and Identity)* (Frankfurt, a. M. [u.a]: Vervuert [u.a.], 1994), p. 49ff.

Johnson-Hill, Jack A., *I-Sight: The World of Rastafari: An Interpretive Sociological Account of Rastafarian Ethics* (Latham, MD: Scarecrow Press, 1995).

Lee, Hélène, *The First Rasta: Leonard Howell and the Rise of Rastafarianism* (Chicago, IL: Lawrence Hill Books, 2003).

Mack, Douglas R. A., *From Babylon to Rastafari: Origin and History of Rastafarian Movement* (Chicago, IL: Frontline Distribution International, 1999).

Murrell, N. Samuel, William D. Spencer, and Adrian A. McFarlance, *Chanting Down Babylon: A Rastafari Reader* (Philadelphia: Temple University Press, 1988).

Nettleford, Rex, *Mirror Mirror: Identity, Race and Protest in Jamaica* (Kingston, Jamaica: Collins and Sangster's, 1970).

Owens, Joseph, *Dread: The Rastafarians of Jamaica* (Kingston, Jamaica: Sangster's, 1976).

Pollard, Velma, *Dread Talk: The Language of Rastafari*, revised edn. (Montreal: McGill-Queen's University Press, 2000).

Poupeye, Veerle, *Caribbean Art* (London: Thames and Hudson, 1998).

Price, Charles, *Becoming Rasta: Origins of Rastafari Identity in Jamaica* (New York: New York University Press, 2009).

Rodney, Walter, *The Groundings with My Brothers* (London: Bgle-L'Ouverture Publications, 1969).

Rogers, Robert Athlyi, *The Holy Piby* (Chicago: Research Associates School Times Publications, 2000; first published in 1924).

Simpson, George Eaton, 'Political Cultism in Western Kingston', *Social and Economic Studies*, 5 (1955): 133–49.

Smith, M. G., Roy Augier, and Rex Nettleford, 'Report on the Rastafari Movement in Kingston, Jamaica' (Mona, Jamaica: Institute of Social and Economic Research, University College of the West Indies, 1960).

Spencer, William David, *Dread Jesus* (London: Society for Promoting Christian Knowledge, 1999).

Sterling, Marvin D., *Babylon East: Performing Dancehall, Roots Reggae and Rastafari in Japan* (Durham: Duke University Press, 2010).

Waters, Anita, *Race, Class and Political Symbols: Reggae and Rastafari in Jamaican Politics* (New Brunswick, NJ: Transaction, 1985).

Zips, Werner (ed.), *Rastafari: A Universal Philosophy in the Third Millennium* (Kingston: Jamaica: Ian Randle, 2006).

Yawney, Carole, 'Dread Wasteland: Rastafarian Ritual in West Kingston, Jamaica', in N. Ross Crumrime (ed.), *Ritual, Symbolism and Ceremonialism in the Americas: Studies in Symbolic Anthropology* (Greenley, CO: Museum of Anthropology, University of Northern Colorado, 1978).

—— 'Moving with the Dawtas of Rastafari: From Myth to Reality', in Terisa E. Turner with Bryan J. Ferguson (eds.), *Arise Ye Mighty People? Gender, Class and Race in Popular Struggles* (Trenton, NJ: African World Press, 1994), 65–74.

—— 'Rasta Mek a Trod: Symbolic Ambiguity in a Globalizing Religion', in Terisa E. Turner with Bryan J. Ferguson (eds.), *Arise Ye Mighty People?: Gender, Class and Race in Popular Struggles* (Trenton, NJ: African World Press, 1994), 75–84.

—— 'Tell Out King Rasta Doctrine around the World: Rastafari in Global Perspectives', in Alvina Ruprecht and Celia Taiana (eds.), *The Reordering of Culture: Latin America, the Caribbean, and Canada in the Hood* (Ottawa: Carleton Press, 1995), 57–74.

—— 'To Grow a Daughter: Cultural Liberation and the Dynamics of Oppression in Jamaica', in A. Miles and G. Finn (eds.), *Feminism in Canada* (Montreal: Black Rose, 1983), 119–44.

—— 'Rastafarian Sistren by the Rivers of Babylon', *Canadian Women Studies*, 5. No. 2 (Winter 1983): 73–75.

Websites

www.Africaspeaks.com
www.Bobmarley.com
www.fulfilledrastafari.org
www.houseofbobo.com
www.Jah.com
www.Rastafarian.net
www.rastafari.org.nz
www.rastafarispeaks.com
www.rastafariwestmidlands.co.uk
www.rastatimes.com

Index

Rastafari

Expand your collection of
VERY SHORT INTRODUCTIONS